W9-BYZ-171

Grade **3**

KUMON MATH WORKBOOKS

Division

Table of Contents

KUM☺N

1 Multiply.

(1) $2 \times 5 =$

(2) $3 \times 5 =$

(3) $4 \times 5 =$

(4) $5 \times 5 =$

(5) $2 \times 6 =$

(6) $3 \times 6 =$

(7) $4 \times 6 =$

(8) $5 \times 6 =$

(9) $2 \times 7 =$

(10) $3 \times 7 =$

(11) $4 \times 7 =$

(12) $5 \times 7 =$

(13) $3 \times 1 =$

(14) $3 \times 2 =$

(15) $3 \times 3 =$

(16) $3 \times 4 =$

(17) $2 \times 1 =$

(18) $2 \times 2 =$

(19) $2 \times 3 =$

(20) $2 \times 4 =$

(21) $5 \times 1 =$

(22) $5 \times 2 =$

(23) $5 \times 3 =$

(24) $5 \times 4 =$

(25) $4 \times 1 =$

(26) $4 \times 2 =$

(27) $4 \times 3 =$

(28) $4 \times 4 =$

(29) $2 \times 8 =$

(30) $2 \times 9 =$

(31) $2 \times 0 =$

(32) $4 \times 8 =$

(33) $4 \times 9 =$

(34) $4 \times 0 =$

(35) $3 \times 8 =$

(36) $3 \times 9 =$

(37) $3 \times 0 =$

(38) $5 \times 8 =$

(39) $5 \times 9 =$

(40) $5 \times 0 =$

(2) Multiply.

2 points per question

(1) $4 \times 6 =$

(2) $2 \times 3 =$

(3) $5 \times 8 =$

(4) $3 \times 5 =$

(5) $4 \times 3 =$

(6) $5 \times 4 =$

(7) $2 \times 7 =$

(8) $3 \times 1 =$

(9) $5 \times 9 =$

(10) $2 \times 4 =$

(11) $4 \times 0 =$

(12) $3 \times 8 =$

(13) $4 \times 4 =$

(14) $2 \times 6 =$

(15) $5 \times 1 =$

(16) $3 \times 3 =$

(17) $2 \times 9 =$

(18) $4 \times 2 =$

(19) $5 \times 7 =$

(20) $3 \times 0 =$

(21) $4 \times 8 =$

(22) $2 \times 5 =$

(23) $5 \times 6 =$

(24) $3 \times 9 =$

(25) $4 \times 1 =$

(26) $2 \times 8 =$

(27) $3 \times 7 =$

(28) $5 \times 3 =$

(29) $2 \times 2 =$

(30) $4 \times 9 =$

Do you remember your multiplication?

Multiplication Review

Level ☆

Date / /

Name

Score /100

1 Multiply.

1 point per question

(1) $6 \times 5 =$

(2) $7 \times 5 =$

(3) $8 \times 5 =$

(4) $9 \times 5 =$

(5) $6 \times 6 =$

(6) $7 \times 6 =$

(7) $8 \times 6 =$

(8) $9 \times 6 =$

(9) $6 \times 7 =$

(10) $7 \times 7 =$

(11) $8 \times 7 =$

(12) $9 \times 7 =$

(13) $7 \times 1 =$

(14) $7 \times 2 =$

(15) $7 \times 3 =$

(16) $7 \times 4 =$

(17) $6 \times 1 =$

(18) $6 \times 2 =$

(19) $6 \times 3 =$

(20) $6 \times 4 =$

(21) $9 \times 1 =$

(22) $9 \times 2 =$

(23) $9 \times 3 =$

(24) $9 \times 4 =$

(25) $8 \times 1 =$

(26) $8 \times 2 =$

(27) $8 \times 3 =$

(28) $8 \times 4 =$

(29) $6 \times 8 =$

(30) $6 \times 9 =$

(31) $6 \times 0 =$

(32) $8 \times 8 =$

(33) $8 \times 9 =$

(34) $8 \times 0 =$

(35) $7 \times 8 =$

(36) $7 \times 9 =$

(37) $7 \times 0 =$

(38) $9 \times 8 =$

(39) $9 \times 9 =$

(40) $9 \times 0 =$

② Multiply.

2 points per question

(1) 8 × 6 =

(2) 6 × 3 =

(3) 9 × 8 =

(4) 7 × 5 =

(5) 8 × 3 =

(6) 9 × 4 =

(7) 6 × 7 =

(8) 7 × 1 =

(9) 9 × 9 =

(10) 6 × 4 =

(11) 8 × 0 =

(12) 7 × 8 =

(13) 8 × 4 =

(14) 6 × 6 =

(15) 9 × 1 =

(16) 7 × 3 =

(17) 6 × 9 =

(18) 8 × 2 =

(19) 9 × 7 =

(20) 7 × 0 =

(21) 8 × 8 =

(22) 6 × 5 =

(23) 9 × 6 =

(24) 7 × 9 =

(25) 8 × 1 =

(26) 6 × 8 =

(27) 7 × 7 =

(28) 9 × 3 =

(29) 6 × 2 =

(30) 8 × 9 =

Don't forget to check your answers when you're done.

3 Multiplication Review

Level ☆

Date   /   /

Name

Score
/100

1 Multiply.

1 point per question

(1) $4 \times 6 =$

(2) $4 \times 5 =$

(3) $4 \times 4 =$

(4) $7 \times 9 =$

(5) $7 \times 8 =$

(6) $7 \times 7 =$

(7) $2 \times 6 =$

(8) $2 \times 5 =$

(9) $2 \times 4 =$

(10) $8 \times 3 =$

(11) $8 \times 2 =$

(12) $8 \times 1 =$

(13) $8 \times 0 =$

(14) $3 \times 9 =$

(15) $3 \times 8 =$

(16) $3 \times 7 =$

(17) $6 \times 6 =$

(18) $6 \times 5 =$

(19) $6 \times 4 =$

(20) $5 \times 9 =$

(21) $5 \times 8 =$

(22) $5 \times 7 =$

(23) $9 \times 3 =$

(24) $9 \times 2 =$

(25) $9 \times 1 =$

(26) $9 \times 0 =$

(27) $4 \times 9 =$

(28) $4 \times 8 =$

(29) $4 \times 7 =$

(30) $7 \times 5 =$

(31) $7 \times 3 =$

(32) $7 \times 1 =$

(33) $2 \times 9 =$

(34) $2 \times 8 =$

(35) $2 \times 7 =$

(36) $8 \times 8 =$

(37) $8 \times 7 =$

(38) $8 \times 6 =$

(39) $3 \times 6 =$

(40) $3 \times 5 =$

(41) $3 \times 4 =$

(42) $6 \times 9 =$

(43) $6 \times 8 =$

(44) $6 \times 7 =$

(45) $5 \times 6 =$

(46) $5 \times 4 =$

(47) $5 \times 2 =$

(48) $9 \times 5 =$

(49) $9 \times 7 =$

(50) $9 \times 9 =$

② Multiply.

1 point per question

(1) $5 \times 2 =$

(2) $3 \times 5 =$

(3) $7 \times 8 =$

(4) $9 \times 1 =$

(5) $4 \times 7 =$

(6) $6 \times 3 =$

(7) $8 \times 6 =$

(8) $2 \times 4 =$

(9) $9 \times 8 =$

(10) $3 \times 3 =$

(11) $5 \times 5 =$

(12) $7 \times 7 =$

(13) $2 \times 2 =$

(14) $8 \times 4 =$

(15) $6 \times 9 =$

(16) $4 \times 6 =$

(17) $5 \times 8 =$

(18) $3 \times 1 =$

(19) $7 \times 5 =$

(20) $9 \times 3 =$

(21) $4 \times 4 =$

(22) $6 \times 7 =$

(23) $8 \times 2 =$

(24) $2 \times 9 =$

(25) $9 \times 6 =$

(26) $3 \times 7 =$

(27) $5 \times 0 =$

(28) $7 \times 3 =$

(29) $2 \times 5 =$

(30) $8 \times 8 =$

(31) $6 \times 4 =$

(32) $4 \times 9 =$

(33) $5 \times 6 =$

(34) $3 \times 2 =$

(35) $7 \times 4 =$

(36) $9 \times 5 =$

(37) $4 \times 1 =$

(38) $6 \times 8 =$

(39) $8 \times 3 =$

(40) $2 \times 6 =$

(41) $9 \times 7 =$

(42) $3 \times 8 =$

(43) $5 \times 4 =$

(44) $7 \times 6 =$

(45) $2 \times 3 =$

(46) $8 \times 5 =$

(47) $6 \times 6 =$

(48) $4 \times 3 =$

(49) $5 \times 7 =$

(50) $9 \times 9 =$

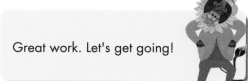

Great work. Let's get going!

1 Write the appropriate number in each box.

1 point per question

(1) $3 \times 7 = 7 \times \boxed{}$

(2) $4 \times 6 = \boxed{} \times 4$

(3) $5 \times \boxed{} = 8 \times 5$

(4) $\boxed{} \times 9 = 9 \times 6$

(5) $3 \times 1 = 1 \times \boxed{}$

(6) $4 \times 1 = \boxed{} \times 4$

(7) $5 \times \boxed{} = 1 \times 5$

(8) $6 \times 0 = \boxed{} \times 6$

(9) $7 \times \boxed{} = 0 \times 7$

(10) $8 \times 0 = \boxed{} \times 8$

2 Multiply.

1 point per question

(1) $2 \times 1 =$

(2) $1 \times 2 =$

(3) $3 \times 1 =$

(4) $1 \times 3 =$

(5) $2 \times 0 =$

(6) $0 \times 2 =$

(7) $3 \times 0 =$

(8) $0 \times 3 =$

(9) $4 \times 1 =$

(10) $1 \times 4 =$

(11) $5 \times 1 =$

(12) $1 \times 5 =$

(13) $4 \times 0 =$

(14) $0 \times 4 =$

(15) $5 \times 0 =$

(16) $0 \times 5 =$

(17) $6 \times 1 =$

(18) $1 \times 6 =$

(19) $6 \times 0 =$

(20) $0 \times 6 =$

(21) $1 \times 7 =$

(22) $0 \times 8 =$

(23) $1 \times 9 =$

(24) $0 \times 7 =$

(25) $1 \times 8 =$

(26) $0 \times 9 =$

(27) $1 \times 1 =$

(28) $0 \times 1 =$

(29) $1 \times 0 =$

(30) $0 \times 0 =$

③ Multiply.

(1) $6 \times 3 =$

(2) $1 \times 5 =$

(3) $4 \times 8 =$

(4) $7 \times 6 =$

(5) $0 \times 2 =$

(6) $8 \times 4 =$

(7) $3 \times 9 =$

(8) $1 \times 7 =$

(9) $9 \times 5 =$

(10) $2 \times 4 =$

(11) $0 \times 8 =$

(12) $5 \times 5 =$

(13) $6 \times 7 =$

(14) $1 \times 3 =$

(15) $4 \times 6 =$

(16) $7 \times 9 =$

(17) $0 \times 4 =$

(18) $8 \times 8 =$

(19) $3 \times 5 =$

(20) $1 \times 1 =$

(21) $9 \times 3 =$

(22) $2 \times 6 =$

(23) $0 \times 9 =$

(24) $5 \times 2 =$

(25) $6 \times 8 =$

(26) $1 \times 4 =$

(27) $4 \times 3 =$

(28) $7 \times 5 =$

(29) $0 \times 7 =$

(30) $8 \times 5 =$

(31) $3 \times 7 =$

(32) $1 \times 6 =$

(33) $9 \times 8 =$

(34) $2 \times 2 =$

(35) $0 \times 6 =$

(36) $5 \times 8 =$

(37) $6 \times 0 =$

(38) $1 \times 2 =$

(39) $4 \times 7 =$

(40) $7 \times 3 =$

(41) $0 \times 0 =$

(42) $8 \times 7 =$

(43) $3 \times 4 =$

(44) $1 \times 9 =$

(45) $9 \times 4 =$

(46) $2 \times 7 =$

(47) $0 \times 3 =$

(48) $5 \times 9 =$

(49) $6 \times 5 =$

(50) $1 \times 0 =$

(51) $4 \times 4 =$

(52) $7 \times 8 =$

(53) $0 \times 5 =$

(54) $8 \times 9 =$

(55) $3 \times 6 =$

(56) $1 \times 8 =$

(57) $9 \times 9 =$

(58) $2 \times 3 =$

(59) $0 \times 1 =$

(60) $5 \times 7 =$

Nice work! Now let's check your score.

Multiplication Review

5

Level ☆

Score

Date / /

Name

/100

1 Multiply.

1 point per question

(1) $2 \times 9 =$

(2) $2 \times 10 =$

(3) $5 \times 9 =$

(4) $5 \times 10 =$

(5) $4 \times 9 =$

(6) $4 \times 10 =$

(7) $6 \times 9 =$

(8) $6 \times 10 =$

(9) $8 \times 9 =$

(10) $8 \times 10 =$

(11) $3 \times 9 =$

(12) $3 \times 10 =$

(13) $7 \times 9 =$

(14) $7 \times 10 =$

(15) $9 \times 9 =$

(16) $9 \times 10 =$

(17) $10 \times 10 =$

(18) $1 \times 9 =$

(19) $1 \times 10 =$

(20) $10 \times 1 =$

(21) $10 \times 2 =$

(22) $10 \times 5 =$

(23) $10 \times 4 =$

(24) $10 \times 6 =$

(25) $10 \times 8 =$

(26) $10 \times 3 =$

(27) $10 \times 7 =$

(28) $10 \times 9 =$

(29) $10 \times 10 =$

(30) $10 \times 2 =$

(31) $10 \times 1 =$

(32) $10 \times 0 =$

(33) $3 \times 10 =$

(34) $10 \times 3 =$

(35) $7 \times 10 =$

(36) $10 \times 7 =$

(37) $8 \times 10 =$

(38) $4 \times 10 =$

(39) $10 \times 2 =$

(40) $10 \times 6 =$

(41) $6 \times 10 =$

(42) $5 \times 10 =$

(43) $10 \times 4 =$

(44) $1 \times 10 =$

(45) $0 \times 10 =$

(46) $10 \times 9 =$

(47) $10 \times 8 =$

(48) $10 \times 10 =$

(49) $2 \times 10 =$

(50) $10 \times 1 =$

② Multiply.

(1) $9 \times 3 =$

(2) $3 \times 10 =$

(3) $7 \times 4 =$

(4) $5 \times 10 =$

(5) $0 \times 6 =$

(6) $6 \times 8 =$

(7) $10 \times 7 =$

(8) $8 \times 9 =$

(9) $2 \times 10 =$

(10) $10 \times 8 =$

(11) $9 \times 0 =$

(12) $5 \times 3 =$

(13) $10 \times 1 =$

(14) $6 \times 7 =$

(15) $6 \times 10 =$

(16) $9 \times 10 =$

(17) $8 \times 4 =$

(18) $10 \times 3 =$

(19) $8 \times 10 =$

(20) $9 \times 7 =$

(21) $2 \times 7 =$

(22) $10 \times 4 =$

(23) $7 \times 10 =$

(24) $6 \times 9 =$

(25) $10 \times 6 =$

(26) $4 \times 8 =$

(27) $0 \times 4 =$

(28) $10 \times 2 =$

(29) $3 \times 6 =$

(30) $10 \times 5 =$

(31) $1 \times 10 =$

(32) $10 \times 0 =$

(33) $7 \times 6 =$

(34) $10 \times 10 =$

(35) $8 \times 7 =$

(36) $5 \times 9 =$

(37) $10 \times 9 =$

(38) $7 \times 3 =$

(39) $0 \times 10 =$

(40) $9 \times 9 =$

(41) $1 \times 8 =$

(42) $10 \times 10 =$

(43) $8 \times 8 =$

(44) $9 \times 10 =$

(45) $4 \times 10 =$

(46) $2 \times 0 =$

(47) $7 \times 8 =$

(48) $9 \times 6 =$

(49) $10 \times 7 =$

(50) $2 \times 9 =$

Let's keep practicing our multiplication!

6 Multiplication Review

Date   /   /   Name

/100

1 Multiply.

1 point per question

(1) $7 \times 3 =$

(2) $4 \times 5 =$

(3) $6 \times 8 =$

(4) $1 \times 3 =$

(5) $5 \times 2 =$

(6) $9 \times 6 =$

(7) $0 \times 7 =$

(8) $2 \times 4 =$

(9) $8 \times 1 =$

(10) $3 \times 6 =$

(11) $7 \times 9 =$

(12) $4 \times 1 =$

(13) $6 \times 0 =$

(14) $1 \times 8 =$

(15) $5 \times 5 =$

(16) $9 \times 2 =$

(17) $0 \times 5 =$

(18) $2 \times 7 =$

(19) $8 \times 6 =$

(20) $3 \times 2 =$

(21) $7 \times 4 =$

(22) $4 \times 0 =$

(23) $6 \times 3 =$

(24) $1 \times 1 =$

(25) $5 \times 9 =$

(26) $9 \times 7 =$

(27) $0 \times 2 =$

(28) $2 \times 6 =$

(29) $8 \times 4 =$

(30) $3 \times 8 =$

(31) $7 \times 0 =$

(32) $4 \times 7 =$

(33) $6 \times 5 =$

(34) $1 \times 2 =$

(35) $5 \times 6 =$

(36) $9 \times 3 =$

(37) $0 \times 9 =$

(38) $2 \times 5 =$

(39) $8 \times 8 =$

(40) $3 \times 4 =$

(41) $7 \times 7 =$

(42) $4 \times 2 =$

(43) $6 \times 7 =$

(44) $1 \times 5 =$

(45) $5 \times 3 =$

(46) $9 \times 8 =$

(47) $0 \times 4 =$

(48) $2 \times 2 =$

(49) $8 \times 5 =$

(50) $3 \times 0 =$

(51) $7 \times 6 =$

(52) $4 \times 9 =$

(53) $6 \times 2 =$

(54) $1 \times 7 =$

(55) $5 \times 8 =$

(56) $9 \times 1 =$

(57) $0 \times 8 =$

(58) $2 \times 1 =$

(59) $8 \times 3 =$

(60) $3 \times 9 =$

2 Multiply.

1 point per question

(1) $7 \times 5 =$

(2) $4 \times 3 =$

(3) $6 \times 9 =$

(4) $1 \times 4 =$

(5) $5 \times 7 =$

(6) $9 \times 4 =$

(7) $0 \times 0 =$

(8) $10 \times 2 =$

(9) $8 \times 7 =$

(10) $3 \times 5 =$

(11) $7 \times 1 =$

(12) $4 \times 6 =$

(13) $6 \times 10 =$

(14) $1 \times 9 =$

(15) $10 \times 3 =$

(16) $9 \times 5 =$

(17) $0 \times 6 =$

(18) $2 \times 3 =$

(19) $8 \times 9 =$

(20) $4 \times 10 =$

(21) $7 \times 8 =$

(22) $10 \times 5 =$

(23) $6 \times 6 =$

(24) $1 \times 0 =$

(25) $5 \times 4 =$

(26) $9 \times 0 =$

(27) $0 \times 10 =$

(28) $2 \times 9 =$

(29) $8 \times 0 =$

(30) $7 \times 10 =$

(31) $7 \times 2 =$

(32) $4 \times 8 =$

(33) $10 \times 10 =$

(34) $1 \times 6 =$

(35) $5 \times 1 =$

(36) $9 \times 9 =$

(37) $0 \times 1 =$

(38) $9 \times 10 =$

(39) $8 \times 2 =$

(40) $10 \times 8 =$

Now let's try something a bit different!

7 Inverse Multiplication

Date / /

Name

Score /100

1 Write the appropriate number in each box.

1 point per question

(1) $2 \times \boxed{} = 6$

(2) $2 \times \boxed{} = 8$

(3) $2 \times \boxed{} = 14$

(4) $2 \times \boxed{} = 16$

(5) $2 \times \boxed{} = 4$

(6) $2 \times \boxed{} = 10$

(7) $2 \times \boxed{} = 18$

(8) $2 \times \boxed{} = 0$

(9) $2 \times \boxed{} = 12$

(10) $2 \times \boxed{} = 2$

(11) $3 \times \boxed{} = 15$

(12) $3 \times \boxed{} = 24$

(13) $3 \times \boxed{} = 18$

(14) $3 \times \boxed{} = 21$

(15) $4 \times \boxed{} = 28$

(16) $4 \times \boxed{} = 12$

(17) $4 \times \boxed{} = 24$

(18) $4 \times \boxed{} = 32$

(19) $5 \times \boxed{} = 40$

(20) $5 \times \boxed{} = 0$

(21) $5 \times \boxed{} = 35$

(22) $5 \times \boxed{} = 45$

(23) $6 \times \boxed{} = 36$

(24) $6 \times \boxed{} = 54$

(25) $6 \times \boxed{} = 30$

(26) $6 \times \boxed{} = 42$

(27) $7 \times \boxed{} = 56$

(28) $7 \times \boxed{} = 7$

(29) $7 \times \boxed{} = 63$

(30) $7 \times \boxed{} = 49$

(31) $8 \times \boxed{} = 72$

(32) $8 \times \boxed{} = 16$

(33) $8 \times \boxed{} = 64$

(34) $8 \times \boxed{} = 40$

(35) $9 \times \boxed{} = 63$

(36) $9 \times \boxed{} = 54$

(37) $9 \times \boxed{} = 81$

(38) $10 \times \boxed{} = 70$

(39) $10 \times \boxed{} = 40$

(40) $10 \times \boxed{} = 90$

2 Write the appropriate number in each box.

2 points per question

(1) ☐ × 2 = 4

(2) ☐ × 2 = 6

(3) ☐ × 2 = 18

(4) ☐ × 2 = 14

(5) ☐ × 3 = 9

(6) ☐ × 3 = 12

(7) ☐ × 3 = 24

(8) ☐ × 3 = 18

(9) ☐ × 4 = 16

(10) ☐ × 4 = 8

(11) ☐ × 4 = 28

(12) ☐ × 4 = 12

(13) ☐ × 5 = 25

(14) ☐ × 5 = 10

(15) ☐ × 5 = 45

(16) ☐ × 6 = 18

(17) ☐ × 6 = 54

(18) ☐ × 6 = 42

(19) ☐ × 7 = 28

(20) ☐ × 7 = 56

(21) ☐ × 7 = 35

(22) ☐ × 8 = 64

(23) ☐ × 8 = 16

(24) ☐ × 8 = 40

(25) ☐ × 9 = 81

(26) ☐ × 9 = 9

(27) ☐ × 9 = 36

(28) ☐ × 10 = 80

(29) ☐ × 10 = 30

(30) ☐ × 10 = 60

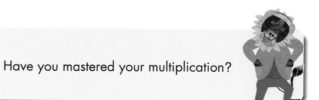

Have you mastered your multiplication?

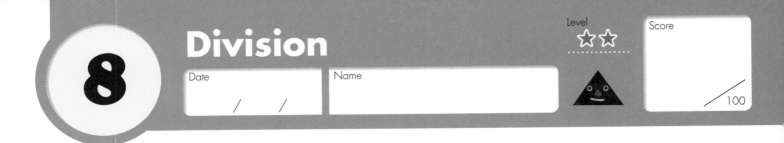

1 Look at the example, and then write the appropriate number in each box below.

4 points per question

Example

Multiplication

$2 \times \boxed{3} = 6$

$3 \times \boxed{4} = 12$

Division

$6 \div 2 = \boxed{3}$

$12 \div 3 = \boxed{4}$

(1) $2 \times \boxed{} = 8$ $8 \div 2 = \boxed{}$ (8) $5 \times \boxed{} = 40$ $40 \div 5 = \boxed{}$

(2) $2 \times \boxed{} = 12$ $12 \div 2 = \boxed{}$ (9) $6 \times \boxed{} = 42$ $42 \div 6 = \boxed{}$

(3) $3 \times \boxed{} = 15$ $15 \div 3 = \boxed{}$ (10) $7 \times \boxed{} = 21$ $21 \div 7 = \boxed{}$

(4) $3 \times \boxed{} = 18$ $18 \div 3 = \boxed{}$ (11) $8 \times \boxed{} = 48$ $48 \div 8 = \boxed{}$

(5) $4 \times \boxed{} = 24$ $24 \div 4 = \boxed{}$ (12) $9 \times \boxed{} = 63$ $63 \div 9 = \boxed{}$

(6) $4 \times \boxed{} = 36$ $36 \div 4 = \boxed{}$ (13) $10 \times \boxed{} = 60$ $60 \div 10 = \boxed{}$

(7) $5 \times \boxed{} = 25$ $25 \div 5 = \boxed{}$

2 **Look at the example, and then write the appropriate number in each box below.**

4 points per question

Example	Multiplication	Division
	$\boxed{2} \times 3 = 6$	$6 \div 3 = \boxed{2}$
	$\boxed{3} \times 4 = 12$	$12 \div 4 = \boxed{3}$

(1) $\boxed{} \times 2 = 4$ $4 \div 2 = \boxed{}$

(2) $\boxed{} \times 2 = 10$ $10 \div 2 = \boxed{}$

(3) $\boxed{} \times 3 = 21$ $21 \div 3 = \boxed{}$

(4) $\boxed{} \times 3 = 27$ $27 \div 3 = \boxed{}$

(5) $\boxed{} \times 4 = 16$ $16 \div 4 = \boxed{}$

(6) $\boxed{} \times 4 = 32$ $32 \div 4 = \boxed{}$

(7) $\boxed{} \times 5 = 30$ $30 \div 5 = \boxed{}$

(8) $\boxed{} \times 6 = 48$ $48 \div 6 = \boxed{}$

(9) $\boxed{} \times 7 = 35$ $35 \div 7 = \boxed{}$

(10) $\boxed{} \times 8 = 32$ $32 \div 8 = \boxed{}$

(11) $\boxed{} \times 9 = 72$ $72 \div 9 = \boxed{}$

(12) $\boxed{} \times 10 = 80$ $80 \div 10 = \boxed{}$

Don't forget to check your answers when you're done.

Division

Date　　/　　/

Name

Level ★★

Score
/100

1 Divide.

2 points per question

(1)　8 ÷ 2 =

(2)　12 ÷ 2 =

(3)　16 ÷ 2 =

(4)　6 ÷ 2 =

(5)　4 ÷ 2 =

(6)　2 ÷ 2 =

(7)　10 ÷ 2 =

(8)　18 ÷ 2 =

(9)　14 ÷ 2 =

(10)　0 ÷ 2 =

(11)　6 ÷ 3 =

(12)　15 ÷ 3 =

(13)　21 ÷ 3 =

(14)　3 ÷ 3 =

(15)　24 ÷ 3 =

(16)　18 ÷ 3 =

(17)　0 ÷ 3 =

(18)　27 ÷ 3 =

(19)　8 ÷ 4 =

(20)　24 ÷ 4 =

(21)　16 ÷ 4 =

(22)　28 ÷ 4 =

(23)　0 ÷ 4 =

(24)　36 ÷ 4 =

(25)　20 ÷ 4 =

If zero is divided by anything, the answer is always zero.

2 **Divide.**

(1) $12 \div 4 =$

(2) $8 \div 4 =$

(3) $28 \div 4 =$

(4) $16 \div 4 =$

(5) $4 \div 4 =$

(6) $0 \div 4 =$

(7) $32 \div 4 =$

(8) $10 \div 5 =$

(9) $25 \div 5 =$

(10) $30 \div 5 =$

(11) $0 \div 5 =$

(12) $15 \div 5 =$

(13) $40 \div 5 =$

(14) $35 \div 5 =$

(15) $45 \div 5 =$

(16) $20 \div 5 =$

(17) $18 \div 6 =$

(18) $42 \div 6 =$

(19) $30 \div 6 =$

(20) $24 \div 6 =$

(21) $48 \div 6 =$

(22) $0 \div 6 =$

(23) $36 \div 6 =$

(24) $6 \div 6 =$

(25) $54 \div 6 =$

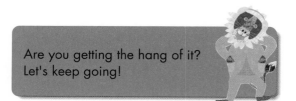

Are you getting the hang of it?
Let's keep going!

Division

1   Divide.

2 points per question

(1) $8 \div 2 =$

(2) $16 \div 2 =$

(3) $4 \div 2 =$

(4) $2 \div 2 =$

(5) $18 \div 2 =$

(6) $10 \div 2 =$

(7) $9 \div 3 =$

(8) $15 \div 3 =$

(9) $24 \div 3 =$

(10) $6 \div 3 =$

(11) $18 \div 3 =$

(12) $21 \div 3 =$

(13) $27 \div 3 =$

(14) $20 \div 4 =$

(15) $8 \div 4 =$

(16) $4 \div 4 =$

(17) $32 \div 4 =$

(18) $28 \div 4 =$

(19) $36 \div 4 =$

(20) $30 \div 5 =$

(21) $15 \div 5 =$

(22) $40 \div 5 =$

(23) $5 \div 5 =$

(24) $20 \div 5 =$

(25) $35 \div 5 =$

2 Divide.

(1) $15 \div 5 =$

(2) $40 \div 5 =$

(3) $35 \div 5 =$

(4) $10 \div 5 =$

(5) $25 \div 5 =$

(6) $5 \div 5 =$

(7) $6 \div 6 =$

(8) $36 \div 6 =$

(9) $12 \div 6 =$

(10) $30 \div 6 =$

(11) $54 \div 6 =$

(12) $18 \div 6 =$

(13) $42 \div 6 =$

(14) $28 \div 7 =$

(15) $14 \div 7 =$

(16) $49 \div 7 =$

(17) $7 \div 7 =$

(18) $35 \div 7 =$

(19) $63 \div 7 =$

(20) $16 \div 8 =$

(21) $40 \div 8 =$

(22) $24 \div 8 =$

(23) $8 \div 8 =$

(24) $32 \div 8 =$

(25) $48 \div 8 =$

If you made a mistake, just try the problem again. You can do it!

Division

Level ★★

Date   /   /

Name

Score   /100

1 Divide.

2 points per question

(1) $18 \div 6 =$

(2) $42 \div 6 =$

(3) $12 \div 6 =$

(4) $48 \div 6 =$

(5) $24 \div 6 =$

(6) $30 \div 6 =$

(7) $14 \div 7 =$

(8) $35 \div 7 =$

(9) $21 \div 7 =$

(10) $56 \div 7 =$

(11) $7 \div 7 =$

(12) $42 \div 7 =$

(13) $28 \div 7 =$

(14) $16 \div 8 =$

(15) $32 \div 8 =$

(16) $56 \div 8 =$

(17) $72 \div 8 =$

(18) $40 \div 8 =$

(19) $18 \div 9 =$

(20) $9 \div 9 =$

(21) $54 \div 9 =$

(22) $27 \div 9 =$

(23) $81 \div 9 =$

(24) $36 \div 9 =$

(25) $72 \div 9 =$

2 Divide.

2 points per question

(1) 10 ÷ 2 =

(2) 18 ÷ 2 =

(3) 6 ÷ 2 =

(4) 15 ÷ 3 =

(5) 24 ÷ 3 =

(6) 9 ÷ 3 =

(7) 20 ÷ 4 =

(8) 36 ÷ 4 =

(9) 12 ÷ 4 =

(10) 8 ÷ 4 =

(11) 25 ÷ 5 =

(12) 40 ÷ 5 =

(13) 45 ÷ 5 =

(14) 24 ÷ 6 =

(15) 6 ÷ 6 =

(16) 42 ÷ 6 =

(17) 21 ÷ 7 =

(18) 63 ÷ 7 =

(19) 14 ÷ 7 =

(20) 48 ÷ 8 =

(21) 16 ÷ 8 =

(22) 72 ÷ 8 =

(23) 18 ÷ 9 =

(24) 45 ÷ 9 =

(25) 63 ÷ 9 =

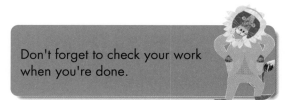

Don't forget to check your work when you're done.

Division

Date / /

Name

Level ★★

Score   /100

1 Divide.

2 points per question

(1) $6 \div 2 =$

(2) $9 \div 3 =$

(3) $8 \div 4 =$

(4) $6 \div 3 =$

(5) $6 \div 6 =$

(6) $14 \div 7 =$

(7) $16 \div 8 =$

(8) $18 \div 9 =$

(9) $8 \div 2 =$

(10) $12 \div 3 =$

(11) $12 \div 4 =$

(12) $15 \div 5 =$

(13) $18 \div 6 =$

(14) $15 \div 3 =$

(15) $20 \div 4 =$

(16) $20 \div 5 =$

(17) $21 \div 7 =$

(18) $32 \div 8 =$

(19) $27 \div 9 =$

(20) $10 \div 2 =$

(21) $18 \div 3 =$

(22) $16 \div 4 =$

(23) $25 \div 5 =$

(24) $30 \div 6 =$

(25) $35 \div 7 =$

② Divide.

2 points per question

(1) $10 \div 2 =$

(2) $18 \div 3 =$

(3) $28 \div 4 =$

(4) $30 \div 5 =$

(5) $36 \div 6 =$

(6) $42 \div 7 =$

(7) $56 \div 8 =$

(8) $63 \div 9 =$

(9) $12 \div 2 =$

(10) $21 \div 3 =$

(11) $25 \div 5 =$

(12) $42 \div 6 =$

(13) $49 \div 7 =$

(14) $24 \div 4 =$

(15) $35 \div 5 =$

(16) $36 \div 6 =$

(17) $56 \div 7 =$

(18) $18 \div 2 =$

(19) $24 \div 3 =$

(20) $32 \div 4 =$

(21) $45 \div 5 =$

(22) $54 \div 6 =$

(23) $63 \div 7 =$

(24) $72 \div 8 =$

(25) $81 \div 9 =$

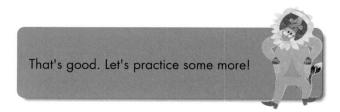

That's good. Let's practice some more!

Division

Date / /

Name

1 Divide.

(1) $8 \div 2 =$

(2) $9 \div 3 =$

(3) $16 \div 4 =$

(4) $16 \div 2 =$

(5) $18 \div 3 =$

(6) $20 \div 4 =$

(7) $20 \div 5 =$

(8) $24 \div 6 =$

(9) $28 \div 7 =$

(10) $32 \div 8 =$

(11) $18 \div 2 =$

(12) $18 \div 3 =$

(13) $24 \div 4 =$

(14) $12 \div 2 =$

(15) $12 \div 3 =$

(16) $16 \div 4 =$

(17) $25 \div 5 =$

(18) $30 \div 6 =$

(19) $15 \div 3 =$

(20) $28 \div 4 =$

(21) $30 \div 5 =$

(22) $42 \div 6 =$

(23) $49 \div 7 =$

(24) $48 \div 8 =$

(25) $54 \div 9 =$

2 Divide.

(1) 12 ÷ 2 =

(2) 21 ÷ 3 =

(3) 32 ÷ 4 =

(4) 45 ÷ 5 =

(5) 24 ÷ 6 =

(6) 49 ÷ 7 =

(7) 32 ÷ 8 =

(8) 27 ÷ 9 =

(9) 10 ÷ 2 =

(10) 24 ÷ 3 =

(11) 36 ÷ 4 =

(12) 40 ÷ 5 =

(13) 48 ÷ 6 =

(14) 30 ÷ 5 =

(15) 42 ÷ 6 =

(16) 28 ÷ 7 =

(17) 40 ÷ 8 =

(18) 18 ÷ 2 =

(19) 27 ÷ 3 =

(20) 28 ÷ 4 =

(21) 35 ÷ 5 =

(22) 54 ÷ 6 =

(23) 56 ÷ 7 =

(24) 72 ÷ 8 =

(25) 81 ÷ 9 =

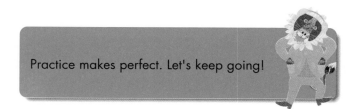

Practice makes perfect. Let's keep going!

Division

1 Divide.

2 points per question

(1) $4 \div 2 =$

(2) $2 \div 2 =$

(3) $2 \div 1 =$

(4) $0 \div 2 =$

(5) $14 \div 2 =$

(6) $15 \div 5 =$

(7) $5 \div 5 =$

(8) $5 \div 1 =$

(9) $12 \div 3 =$

(10) $3 \div 3 =$

(11) $3 \div 1 =$

(12) $21 \div 7 =$

(13) $14 \div 7 =$

(14) $7 \div 7 =$

(15) $7 \div 1 =$

(16) $0 \div 4 =$

(17) $16 \div 4 =$

(18) $4 \div 4 =$

(19) $4 \div 1 =$

(20) $12 \div 6 =$

(21) $6 \div 6 =$

(22) $6 \div 1 =$

(23) $1 \div 1 =$

(24) $0 \div 1 =$

(25) $8 \div 1 =$

2 Divide.

(1) 8 ÷ 1 =

(2) 1 ÷ 1 =

(3) 18 ÷ 9 =

(4) 25 ÷ 5 =

(5) 24 ÷ 8 =

(6) 0 ÷ 8 =

(7) 21 ÷ 7 =

(8) 48 ÷ 6 =

(9) 6 ÷ 6 =

(10) 28 ÷ 7 =

(11) 0 ÷ 7 =

(12) 32 ÷ 8 =

(13) 45 ÷ 9 =

(14) 27 ÷ 9 =

(15) 9 ÷ 9 =

(16) 0 ÷ 9 =

(17) 6 ÷ 1 =

(18) 8 ÷ 8 =

(19) 42 ÷ 7 =

(20) 27 ÷ 3 =

(21) 40 ÷ 8 =

(22) 35 ÷ 7 =

(23) 7 ÷ 7 =

(24) 64 ÷ 8 =

(25) 72 ÷ 9 =

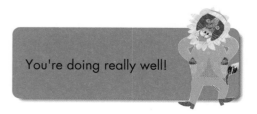

You're doing really well!

Date / /

Name

Level ★★

Score /100

1 Divide.

2 points per question

(1) $12 \div 3 =$

(2) $20 \div 4 =$

(3) $12 \div 6 =$

(4) $20 \div 5 =$

(5) $18 \div 3 =$

(6) $24 \div 4 =$

(7) $18 \div 6 =$

(8) $24 \div 6 =$

(9) $21 \div 3 =$

(10) $27 \div 3 =$

(11) $21 \div 7 =$

(12) $27 \div 9 =$

(13) $25 \div 5 =$

(14) $30 \div 5 =$

(15) $28 \div 4 =$

(16) $30 \div 6 =$

(17) $28 \div 7 =$

(18) $35 \div 7 =$

(19) $32 \div 4 =$

(20) $35 \div 5 =$

(21) $32 \div 8 =$

(22) $36 \div 9 =$

(23) $40 \div 5 =$

(24) $36 \div 4 =$

(25) $40 \div 8 =$

2 Divide.

2 points per question

(1) $32 \div 8 =$

(2) $35 \div 5 =$

(3) $36 \div 9 =$

(4) $32 \div 4 =$

(5) $35 \div 7 =$

(6) $36 \div 6 =$

(7) $40 \div 5 =$

(8) $42 \div 6 =$

(9) $45 \div 5 =$

(10) $40 \div 8 =$

(11) $42 \div 7 =$

(12) $45 \div 9 =$

(13) $49 \div 7 =$

(14) $48 \div 8 =$

(15) $54 \div 6 =$

(16) $64 \div 8 =$

(17) $48 \div 6 =$

(18) $54 \div 9 =$

(19) $56 \div 8 =$

(20) $63 \div 7 =$

(21) $72 \div 9 =$

(22) $56 \div 7 =$

(23) $63 \div 9 =$

(24) $72 \div 8 =$

(25) $81 \div 9 =$

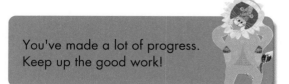

You've made a lot of progress.
Keep up the good work!

Division

1 Divide.

2 points per question

(1) $28 \div 4 =$

(2) $20 \div 5 =$

(3) $24 \div 4 =$

(4) $30 \div 6 =$

(5) $35 \div 5 =$

(6) $32 \div 4 =$

(7) $36 \div 6 =$

(8) $28 \div 7 =$

(9) $20 \div 4 =$

(10) $24 \div 6 =$

(11) $30 \div 5 =$

(12) $35 \div 7 =$

(13) $32 \div 8 =$

(14) $36 \div 4 =$

(15) $40 \div 5 =$

(16) $42 \div 7 =$

(17) $45 \div 9 =$

(18) $48 \div 8 =$

(19) $49 \div 7 =$

(20) $64 \div 8 =$

(21) $36 \div 9 =$

(22) $40 \div 8 =$

(23) $42 \div 6 =$

(24) $45 \div 5 =$

(25) $48 \div 6 =$

② Divide.

2 points per question

(1) $24 \div 6 =$

(2) $30 \div 5 =$

(3) $36 \div 6 =$

(4) $21 \div 7 =$

(5) $35 \div 5 =$

(6) $48 \div 6 =$

(7) $49 \div 7 =$

(8) $48 \div 8 =$

(9) $35 \div 7 =$

(10) $21 \div 3 =$

(11) $36 \div 9 =$

(12) $30 \div 6 =$

(13) $24 \div 8 =$

(14) $42 \div 7 =$

(15) $40 \div 8 =$

(16) $45 \div 5 =$

(17) $54 \div 6 =$

(18) $63 \div 9 =$

(19) $72 \div 8 =$

(20) $72 \div 9 =$

(21) $63 \div 7 =$

(22) $54 \div 9 =$

(23) $45 \div 9 =$

(24) $40 \div 5 =$

(25) $42 \div 6 =$

Don't forget to check your answers when you're done.

Division

Level ★★

Score /100

1 Divide.

2 points per question

(1) $21 \div 3 =$

(2) $18 \div 2 =$

(3) $25 \div 5 =$

(4) $24 \div 6 =$

(5) $16 \div 2 =$

(6) $28 \div 4 =$

(7) $35 \div 7 =$

(8) $36 \div 4 =$

(9) $30 \div 5 =$

(10) $32 \div 4 =$

(11) $28 \div 7 =$

(12) $36 \div 6 =$

(13) $40 \div 8 =$

(14) $20 \div 5 =$

(15) $24 \div 4 =$

(16) $30 \div 6 =$

(17) $35 \div 5 =$

(18) $42 \div 6 =$

(19) $45 \div 5 =$

(20) $49 \div 7 =$

(21) $54 \div 6 =$

(22) $48 \div 8 =$

(23) $56 \div 7 =$

(24) $64 \div 8 =$

(25) $63 \div 7 =$

2 Divide.

2 points per question

(1) $42 \div 6 =$

(2) $49 \div 7 =$

(3) $56 \div 8 =$

(4) $54 \div 9 =$

(5) $36 \div 4 =$

(6) $24 \div 3 =$

(7) $40 \div 5 =$

(8) $56 \div 7 =$

(9) $63 \div 9 =$

(10) $72 \div 8 =$

(11) $54 \div 6 =$

(12) $32 \div 8 =$

(13) $64 \div 8 =$

(14) $35 \div 5 =$

(15) $32 \div 4 =$

(16) $48 \div 8 =$

(17) $27 \div 3 =$

(18) $36 \div 6 =$

(19) $45 \div 9 =$

(20) $28 \div 4 =$

(21) $63 \div 7 =$

(22) $72 \div 9 =$

(23) $42 \div 7 =$

(24) $40 \div 8 =$

(25) $81 \div 9 =$

Well done! Let's try something different now!

18 Division with Remainders ★★

Level

Date / /

Name

Score

/100

1 Solve each word problem.

6 points per question

(1) If 4 pieces of candy are divided equally among 2 children, how many will each child receive?

⟨Show your work.⟩

$$4 \div 2 = \boxed{}$$

⟨Ans.⟩ $\boxed{}$ pieces

(2) If 5 pieces of candy are divided equally among 2 children, how many will each child receive, and how many will remain?

⟨Show your work.⟩

$$5 \div 2 = \boxed{} \ R \ \boxed{}$$

⟨Ans.⟩ $\boxed{}$ pieces with a remainder of $\boxed{}$

(3) If 6 pieces of candy are divided equally among 3 children, how many will each child receive?

⟨Show your work.⟩

$$6 \div 3 = \boxed{}$$

⟨Ans.⟩ $\boxed{}$ pieces

(4) If 7 pieces of candy are divided equally among 3 children, how many will each child receive, and how many will remain?

⟨Show your work.⟩

$$7 \div 3 = \boxed{} \ R \ \boxed{}$$

⟨Ans.⟩ $\boxed{}$ pieces with a remainder of $\boxed{}$

(5) If 8 pieces of candy are divided equally among 3 children, how many will each child receive, and how many will remain?

⟨Show your work.⟩

$$8 \div 3 = \boxed{} \ R \ \boxed{}$$

⟨Ans.⟩ $\boxed{}$ pieces with a remainder of $\boxed{}$

2 Solve each word problem.

10 points per question

(1) If 9 pieces of candy are divided equally among 3 children, how many will each child receive?

〈Show your work.〉

〈**Ans.**〉 ☐ pieces

(2) If 10 pieces of candy are divided equally among 3 children, how many will each child receive, and how many will remain?

〈Show your work.〉

〈**Ans.**〉 ☐ pieces with a remainder of ☐

(3) If 11 pieces of candy are divided equally among 3 children, how many will each child receive, and how many will remain?

〈Show your work.〉

〈**Ans.**〉 ☐ pieces with a remainder of ☐

(4) If 11 pieces of candy are divided equally among 4 children, how many will each child receive, and how many will remain?

〈Show your work.〉

〈**Ans.**〉 ☐ pieces with a remainder of ☐

(5) If 13 pieces of candy are divided equally among 4 children, how many will each child receive, and how many will remain?

〈Show your work.〉

〈**Ans.**〉 ☐ pieces with a remainder of ☐

(6) If 14 pieces of candy are divided equally among 4 children, how many will each child receive, and how many will remain?

〈Show your work.〉

〈**Ans.**〉 ☐ pieces with a remainder of ☐

(7) If 15 pieces of candy are divided equally among 4 children, how many will each child receive, and how many will remain?

〈Show your work.〉

〈**Ans.**〉 ☐ pieces with a remainder of ☐

How did you like these word problems? Not bad, right?

19 Division with Remainders

Date / /

Name

Score /100

1 Divide.

2 points per question

(1) $4 \div 2 = \boxed{}$

(2) $5 \div 2 = \boxed{} \text{R} \boxed{}$

(3) $6 \div 2 = \boxed{}$

(4) $7 \div 2 = \boxed{} \text{R} \boxed{}$

(5) $8 \div 2 =$

(6) $9 \div 2 =$

(7) $10 \div 2 =$

(8) $11 \div 2 =$

(9) $12 \div 2 =$

(10) $13 \div 2 =$

(11) $14 \div 2 =$

(12) $15 \div 2 =$

(13) $16 \div 2 =$

(14) $17 \div 2 =$

(15) $18 \div 2 =$

(16) $19 \div 2 =$

(17) $5 \div 2 =$

(18) $6 \div 2 =$

(19) $7 \div 2 =$

(20) $10 \div 2 =$

(21) $11 \div 2 =$

(22) $12 \div 2 =$

(23) $15 \div 2 =$

(24) $16 \div 2 =$

(25) $17 \div 2 =$

2 Divide.

(1) $6 \div 3 = \boxed{}$

(2) $7 \div 3 = \boxed{} \text{R} \boxed{}$

(3) $8 \div 3 = \boxed{} \text{R} \boxed{}$

(4) $9 \div 3 =$

(5) $10 \div 3 =$

(6) $11 \div 3 =$

(7) $12 \div 3 =$

(8) $13 \div 3 =$

(9) $14 \div 3 =$

(10) $15 \div 3 =$

(11) $16 \div 3 =$

(12) $17 \div 3 =$

(13) $18 \div 3 =$

(14) $19 \div 3 =$

(15) $20 \div 3 =$

(16) $21 \div 3 =$

(17) $22 \div 3 =$

(18) $23 \div 3 =$

(19) $24 \div 3 =$

(20) $25 \div 3 =$

(21) $26 \div 3 =$

(22) $27 \div 3 =$

(23) $28 \div 3 =$

(24) $29 \div 3 =$

(25) $13 \div 3 =$

The remainder should always be smaller than the divisor. On this page the divisor is 3.

If you're not sure about an answer, it never hurts to try again!

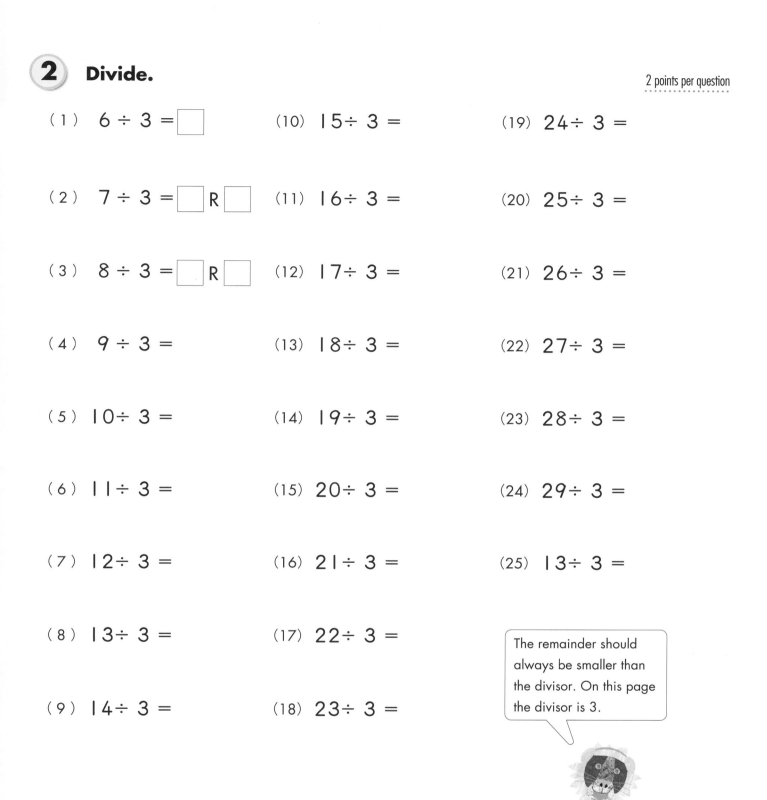

20 Division with Remainders

Level ★★

Date / /

Name

Score /100

1 Divide.

2 points per question

(1) $6 \div 3 =$

(2) $7 \div 3 =$

(3) $8 \div 3 =$

(4) $9 \div 3 =$

(5) $10 \div 3 =$

(6) $6 \div 2 =$

(7) $7 \div 2 =$

(8) $8 \div 2 =$

(9) $9 \div 2 =$

(10) $10 \div 2 =$

(11) $12 \div 3 =$

(12) $13 \div 3 =$

(13) $14 \div 3 =$

(14) $15 \div 3 =$

(15) $16 \div 3 =$

(16) $12 \div 2 =$

(17) $13 \div 2 =$

(18) $14 \div 2 =$

(19) $15 \div 2 =$

(20) $16 \div 2 =$

(21) $18 \div 3 =$

(22) $19 \div 3 =$

(23) $20 \div 3 =$

(24) $21 \div 3 =$

(25) $22 \div 3 =$

2 **Divide.**

(1) $8 \div 4 = \boxed{}$

(2) $9 \div 4 = \boxed{} \text{ R } \boxed{}$

(3) $10 \div 4 =$

(4) $11 \div 4 =$

(5) $12 \div 4 =$

(6) $13 \div 4 =$

(7) $14 \div 4 =$

(8) $15 \div 4 =$

(9) $16 \div 4 =$

(10) $17 \div 4 =$

(11) $18 \div 4 =$

(12) $19 \div 4 =$

(13) $20 \div 4 =$

(14) $21 \div 4 =$

(15) $22 \div 4 =$

(16) $23 \div 4 =$

(17) $24 \div 4 =$

(18) $25 \div 4 =$

(19) $27 \div 4 =$

(20) $28 \div 4 =$

(21) $30 \div 4 =$

(22) $33 \div 4 =$

(23) $36 \div 4 =$

(24) $38 \div 4 =$

(25) $39 \div 4 =$

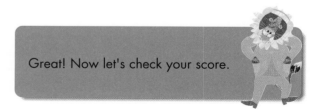

Great! Now let's check your score.

Division with Remainders

Date / /

Name

Score /100

1 Divide.

2 points per question

(1) $10 \div 5 = \boxed{}$

(2) $11 \div 5 = \boxed{} \, R \, \boxed{}$

(3) $12 \div 5 =$

(4) $13 \div 5 =$

(5) $14 \div 5 =$

(6) $15 \div 5 =$

(7) $16 \div 5 =$

(8) $17 \div 5 =$

(9) $18 \div 5 =$

(10) $19 \div 5 =$

(11) $20 \div 5 =$

(12) $21 \div 5 =$

(13) $22 \div 5 =$

(14) $23 \div 5 =$

(15) $25 \div 5 =$

(16) $27 \div 5 =$

(17) $29 \div 5 =$

(18) $30 \div 5 =$

(19) $33 \div 5 =$

(20) $36 \div 5 =$

(21) $39 \div 5 =$

(22) $42 \div 5 =$

(23) $45 \div 5 =$

(24) $47 \div 5 =$

(25) $49 \div 5 =$

2 Divide.

2 points per question

(1) $15 \div 5 =$

(2) $16 \div 5 =$

(3) $17 \div 5 =$

(4) $18 \div 5 =$

(5) $19 \div 5 =$

(6) $16 \div 4 =$

(7) $17 \div 4 =$

(8) $18 \div 4 =$

(9) $19 \div 4 =$

(10) $20 \div 4 =$

(11) $20 \div 5 =$

(12) $21 \div 5 =$

(13) $22 \div 5 =$

(14) $23 \div 5 =$

(15) $24 \div 5 =$

(16) $28 \div 4 =$

(17) $29 \div 4 =$

(18) $30 \div 4 =$

(19) $31 \div 4 =$

(20) $32 \div 4 =$

(21) $25 \div 5 =$

(22) $26 \div 5 =$

(23) $27 \div 5 =$

(24) $28 \div 5 =$

(25) $29 \div 5 =$

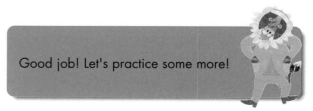

Good job! Let's practice some more!

22 Division with Remainders ★★

Level ★★

Date / /

Name

Score /100

1 Divide.

2 points per question

(1) 4 ÷ 2 =

(2) 7 ÷ 2 =

(3) 10 ÷ 2 =

(4) 13 ÷ 2 =

(5) 16 ÷ 2 =

(6) 19 ÷ 2 =

(7) 6 ÷ 3 =

(8) 10 ÷ 3 =

(9) 14 ÷ 3 =

(10) 18 ÷ 3 =

(11) 22 ÷ 3 =

(12) 26 ÷ 3 =

(13) 8 ÷ 4 =

(14) 13 ÷ 4 =

(15) 18 ÷ 4 =

(16) 23 ÷ 4 =

(17) 28 ÷ 4 =

(18) 33 ÷ 4 =

(19) 38 ÷ 4 =

(20) 10 ÷ 5 =

(21) 16 ÷ 5 =

(22) 22 ÷ 5 =

(23) 28 ÷ 5 =

(24) 34 ÷ 5 =

(25) 40 ÷ 5 =

44 © Kumon Publishing Co., Ltd.

2 **Divide.**

(1) $5 \div 2 =$

(2) $8 \div 2 =$

(3) $11 \div 2 =$

(4) $14 \div 2 =$

(5) $17 \div 2 =$

(6) $19 \div 2 =$

(7) $8 \div 3 =$

(8) $12 \div 3 =$

(9) $16 \div 3 =$

(10) $20 \div 3 =$

(11) $24 \div 3 =$

(12) $28 \div 3 =$

(13) $9 \div 4 =$

(14) $14 \div 4 =$

(15) $19 \div 4 =$

(16) $24 \div 4 =$

(17) $29 \div 4 =$

(18) $34 \div 4 =$

(19) $12 \div 5 =$

(20) $18 \div 5 =$

(21) $24 \div 5 =$

(22) $30 \div 5 =$

(23) $36 \div 5 =$

(24) $42 \div 5 =$

(25) $48 \div 5 =$

Remember, just take it step by step!
You're doing really well!

Division with Remainders

23

Level ★★

Date / /

Name

Score
/ 100

1 Divide.

2 points per question

(1) $6 \div 2 = \boxed{}$

(2) $6 \div 3 = \boxed{}$

(3) $7 \div 2 = \boxed{} R \boxed{}$

(4) $7 \div 3 =$

(5) $8 \div 2 =$

(6) $8 \div 3 =$

(7) $8 \div 4 =$

(8) $9 \div 2 =$

(9) $9 \div 3 =$

(10) $9 \div 4 =$

(11) $9 \div 5 =$

(12) $10 \div 2 = \boxed{}$

(13) $10 \div 3 = \boxed{} R \boxed{}$

(14) $10 \div 4 =$

(15) $10 \div 5 =$

(16) $11 \div 2 =$

(17) $11 \div 3 =$

(18) $11 \div 4 =$

(19) $11 \div 5 =$

(20) $12 \div 2 =$

(21) $12 \div 3 =$

(22) $12 \div 4 =$

(23) $12 \div 5 =$

(24) $13 \div 2 =$

(25) $13 \div 3 =$

46   © Kumon Publishing Co., Ltd.

2 Divide.

2 points per question

(1) $12 \div 2 = \boxed{}$

(2) $12 \div 3 = \boxed{}$

(3) $12 \div 4 = \boxed{}$

(4) $12 \div 5 = \boxed{} \, R \, \boxed{}$

(5) $12 \div 6 =$

(6) $12 \div 7 =$

(7) $13 \div 2 =$

(8) $13 \div 3 =$

(9) $13 \div 4 =$

(10) $13 \div 5 =$

(11) $13 \div 6 =$

(12) $13 \div 7 =$

(13) $14 \div 2 =$

(14) $14 \div 3 =$

(15) $14 \div 4 =$

(16) $14 \div 5 =$

(17) $14 \div 6 =$

(18) $14 \div 7 =$

(19) $15 \div 2 =$

(20) $15 \div 3 =$

(21) $15 \div 4 =$

(22) $15 \div 5 =$

(23) $15 \div 6 =$

(24) $15 \div 7 =$

(25) $15 \div 8 =$

Don't forget to check your answers when you're done.

24 Division with Remainders ★★

Level ★★

Date / /

Name

Score /100

1 **Divide.**

2 points per question

(1) $16 \div 2 =$

(2) $16 \div 3 =$

(3) $16 \div 4 =$

(4) $16 \div 5 =$

(5) $16 \div 6 =$

(6) $16 \div 7 =$

(7) $16 \div 8 =$

(8) $16 \div 9 =$

(9) $17 \div 2 =$

(10) $17 \div 3 =$

(11) $17 \div 4 =$

(12) $17 \div 5 =$

(13) $17 \div 6 =$

(14) $17 \div 7 =$

(15) $17 \div 8 =$

(16) $17 \div 9 =$

(17) $18 \div 2 =$

(18) $18 \div 3 =$

(19) $18 \div 4 =$

(20) $18 \div 5 =$

(21) $18 \div 6 =$

(22) $18 \div 7 =$

(23) $18 \div 8 =$

(24) $18 \div 9 =$

(25) $19 \div 2 =$

2 Divide.

2 points per question

(1) $19 \div 2 =$

(2) $19 \div 3 =$

(3) $19 \div 4 =$

(4) $19 \div 5 =$

(5) $19 \div 6 =$

(6) $19 \div 7 =$

(7) $19 \div 8 =$

(8) $19 \div 9 =$

(9) $20 \div 2 = \boxed{10}$

The answer is larger than 9.

(10) $20 \div 3 =$

(11) $20 \div 4 =$

(12) $20 \div 5 =$

(13) $20 \div 6 =$

(14) $20 \div 7 =$

(15) $20 \div 8 =$

(16) $20 \div 9 =$

(17) $20 \div 2 = \boxed{}$

(18) $21 \div 3 =$

(19) $21 \div 4 =$

(20) $21 \div 5 =$

(21) $21 \div 6 =$

(22) $21 \div 7 =$

(23) $21 \div 8 =$

(24) $21 \div 9 =$

(25) $22 \div 3 =$

If a problem looks tricky, just think about it a bit more!

25 Division with Remainders

Level ★★

Date   /   /

Name

Score   /100

1 Divide.

2 points per question

(1) 22 ÷ 3 =

(2) 22 ÷ 4 =

(3) 22 ÷ 5 =

(4) 22 ÷ 6 =

(5) 22 ÷ 7 =

(6) 22 ÷ 8 =

(7) 22 ÷ 9 =

(8) 23 ÷ 3 =

(9) 23 ÷ 4 =

(10) 23 ÷ 5 =

(11) 23 ÷ 6 =

(12) 23 ÷ 7 =

(13) 23 ÷ 8 =

(14) 23 ÷ 9 =

(15) 24 ÷ 3 =

(16) 24 ÷ 4 =

(17) 24 ÷ 5 =

(18) 24 ÷ 6 =

(19) 24 ÷ 7 =

(20) 24 ÷ 8 =

(21) 24 ÷ 9 =

(22) 25 ÷ 3 =

(23) 25 ÷ 4 =

(24) 25 ÷ 5 =

(25) 25 ÷ 6 =

50   © Kumon Publishing Co., Ltd.

2 Divide.

(1) 25 ÷ 3 =

(2) 25 ÷ 4 =

(3) 25 ÷ 5 =

(4) 25 ÷ 6 =

(5) 25 ÷ 7 =

(6) 25 ÷ 8 =

(7) 25 ÷ 9 =

(8) 26 ÷ 3 =

(9) 26 ÷ 4 =

(10) 26 ÷ 5 =

(11) 26 ÷ 6 =

(12) 26 ÷ 7 =

(13) 26 ÷ 8 =

(14) 26 ÷ 9 =

(15) 27 ÷ 3 =

(16) 27 ÷ 4 =

(17) 27 ÷ 5 =

(18) 27 ÷ 6 =

(19) 27 ÷ 7 =

(20) 27 ÷ 8 =

(21) 27 ÷ 9 =

(22) 28 ÷ 3 =

(23) 28 ÷ 4 =

(24) 28 ÷ 5 =

(25) 28 ÷ 6 =

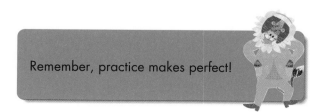

Remember, practice makes perfect!

26 Division with Remainders

Level ★★

Date / /

Name

Score /100

1 **Divide.**

2 points per question

(1) 28 ÷ 4 =

(2) 28 ÷ 5 =

(3) 28 ÷ 6 =

(4) 28 ÷ 7 =

(5) 28 ÷ 8 =

(6) 28 ÷ 9 =

(7) 29 ÷ 3 =

(8) 29 ÷ 4 =

(9) 29 ÷ 5 =

(10) 29 ÷ 6 =

(11) 29 ÷ 7 =

(12) 29 ÷ 8 =

(13) 29 ÷ 9 =

(14) 30 ÷ 3 =

(15) 30 ÷ 4 =

(16) 30 ÷ 5 =

(17) 30 ÷ 6 =

(18) 30 ÷ 7 =

(19) 30 ÷ 8 =

(20) 31 ÷ 4 =

(21) 31 ÷ 5 =

(22) 31 ÷ 6 =

(23) 31 ÷ 7 =

(24) 31 ÷ 8 =

(25) 31 ÷ 9 =

2 Divide.

2 points per question

(1) $32 \div 4 =$

(2) $32 \div 5 =$

(3) $32 \div 6 =$

(4) $32 \div 7 =$

(5) $32 \div 8 =$

(6) $32 \div 9 =$

(7) $33 \div 4 =$

(8) $33 \div 5 =$

(9) $33 \div 6 =$

(10) $33 \div 7 =$

(11) $33 \div 8 =$

(12) $33 \div 9 =$

(13) $34 \div 4 =$

(14) $34 \div 5 =$

(15) $34 \div 6 =$

(16) $34 \div 7 =$

(17) $34 \div 8 =$

(18) $34 \div 9 =$

(19) $35 \div 4 =$

(20) $35 \div 5 =$

(21) $35 \div 6 =$

(22) $35 \div 7 =$

(23) $35 \div 8 =$

(24) $35 \div 9 =$

(25) $36 \div 4 =$

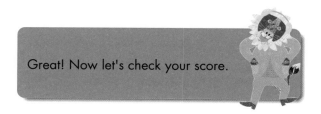

Great! Now let's check your score.

Division with Remainders

Level ★★

Score

Date / /

Name

/100

1 Divide.

2 points per question

(1) 36 ÷ 4 =

(2) 36 ÷ 5 =

(3) 36 ÷ 6 =

(4) 36 ÷ 7 =

(5) 36 ÷ 8 =

(6) 36 ÷ 9 =

(7) 37 ÷ 5 =

(8) 37 ÷ 6 =

(9) 37 ÷ 7 =

(10) 37 ÷ 8 =

(11) 37 ÷ 9 =

(12) 38 ÷ 5 =

(13) 38 ÷ 6 =

(14) 38 ÷ 7 =

(15) 38 ÷ 8 =

(16) 38 ÷ 9 =

(17) 39 ÷ 5 =

(18) 39 ÷ 6 =

(19) 39 ÷ 7 =

(20) 39 ÷ 8 =

(21) 39 ÷ 9 =

(22) 40 ÷ 4 =

(23) 40 ÷ 5 =

(24) 40 ÷ 6 =

(25) 40 ÷ 7 =

2 **Divide.**

2 points per question

(1) 40 ÷ 4 =

(2) 40 ÷ 5 =

(3) 40 ÷ 6 =

(4) 40 ÷ 7 =

(5) 40 ÷ 8 =

(6) 40 ÷ 9 =

(7) 20 ÷ 10 =

(8) 30 ÷ 10 =

(9) 40 ÷ 10 =

(10) 41 ÷ 5 =

(11) 41 ÷ 6 =

(12) 41 ÷ 7 =

(13) 41 ÷ 8 =

(14) 41 ÷ 9 =

(15) 42 ÷ 5 =

(16) 42 ÷ 6 =

(17) 42 ÷ 7 =

(18) 42 ÷ 8 =

(19) 42 ÷ 9 =

(20) 43 ÷ 5 =

(21) 43 ÷ 6 =

(22) 43 ÷ 7 =

(23) 43 ÷ 8 =

(24) 43 ÷ 9 =

(25) 44 ÷ 5 =

Keep up the great work!

28 Division with Remainders ★★

Date / /

Name

Score /100

1 Divide.

2 points per question

(1) $44 \div 5 =$

(2) $44 \div 6 =$

(3) $44 \div 7 =$

(4) $44 \div 8 =$

(5) $44 \div 9 =$

(6) $45 \div 5 =$

(7) $45 \div 6 =$

(8) $45 \div 7 =$

(9) $45 \div 8 =$

(10) $45 \div 9 =$

(11) $46 \div 5 =$

(12) $46 \div 6 =$

(13) $46 \div 7 =$

(14) $46 \div 8 =$

(15) $46 \div 9 =$

(16) $47 \div 5 =$

(17) $47 \div 6 =$

(18) $47 \div 7 =$

(19) $47 \div 8 =$

(20) $47 \div 9 =$

(21) $48 \div 5 =$

(22) $48 \div 6 =$

(23) $48 \div 7 =$

(24) $48 \div 8 =$

(25) $48 \div 9 =$

56   © Kumon Publishing Co., Ltd.

2 Divide.

2 points per question

(1) $49 \div 5 =$

(2) $49 \div 6 =$

(3) $49 \div 7 =$

(4) $49 \div 8 =$

(5) $49 \div 9 =$

(6) $50 \div 5 =$

(7) $50 \div 6 =$

(8) $50 \div 7 =$

(9) $50 \div 8 =$

(10) $50 \div 9 =$

(11) $30 \div 10 =$

(12) $40 \div 10 =$

(13) $50 \div 10 =$

(14) $51 \div 6 =$

(15) $51 \div 7 =$

(16) $51 \div 8 =$

(17) $51 \div 9 =$

(18) $52 \div 6 =$

(19) $52 \div 7 =$

(20) $52 \div 8 =$

(21) $52 \div 9 =$

(22) $53 \div 6 =$

(23) $53 \div 7 =$

(24) $53 \div 8 =$

(25) $53 \div 9 =$

Don't forget to show your parents how far you've come!

29

Division with Remainders ★★

Level ★★

Date　　/　　/

Name

Score

/100

1　Divide.

2 points per question

(1)　$54 \div 6 =$

(2)　$54 \div 7 =$

(3)　$54 \div 8 =$

(4)　$54 \div 9 =$

(5)　$55 \div 6 =$

(6)　$55 \div 7 =$

(7)　$55 \div 8 =$

(8)　$55 \div 9 =$

(9)　$56 \div 6 =$

(10)　$56 \div 7 =$

(11)　$56 \div 8 =$

(12)　$56 \div 9 =$

(13)　$57 \div 6 =$

(14)　$57 \div 7 =$

(15)　$57 \div 8 =$

(16)　$57 \div 9 =$

(17)　$58 \div 6 =$

(18)　$58 \div 7 =$

(19)　$58 \div 8 =$

(20)　$58 \div 9 =$

(21)　$59 \div 6 =$

(22)　$59 \div 7 =$

(23)　$59 \div 8 =$

(24)　$59 \div 9 =$

(25)　$60 \div 6 =$

② Divide.

2 points per question

(1) $60 \div 6 =$

(2) $60 \div 7 =$

(3) $60 \div 8 =$

(4) $60 \div 9 =$

(5) $40 \div 10 =$

(6) $50 \div 10 =$

(7) $60 \div 10 =$

(8) $61 \div 7 =$

(9) $61 \div 8 =$

(10) $61 \div 9 =$

(11) $62 \div 7 =$

(12) $62 \div 8 =$

(13) $62 \div 9 =$

(14) $63 \div 7 =$

(15) $63 \div 8 =$

(16) $63 \div 9 =$

(17) $64 \div 7 =$

(18) $64 \div 8 =$

(19) $64 \div 9 =$

(20) $65 \div 7 =$

(21) $65 \div 8 =$

(22) $65 \div 9 =$

(23) $66 \div 7 =$

(24) $66 \div 8 =$

(25) $66 \div 9 =$

Are you getting the hang of division with remainders?

Division with Remainders

Level ★★

Score

/100

Date / /

Name

1 Divide.

2 points per question

(1) $67 \div 7 =$

(2) $67 \div 8 =$

(3) $67 \div 9 =$

(4) $68 \div 7 =$

(5) $68 \div 8 =$

(6) $68 \div 9 =$

(7) $70 \div 7 =$

(8) $70 \div 8 =$

(9) $70 \div 9 =$

(10) $50 \div 10 =$

(11) $60 \div 10 =$

(12) $70 \div 10 =$

(13) $71 \div 8 =$

(14) $71 \div 9 =$

(15) $72 \div 8 =$

(16) $72 \div 9 =$

(17) $73 \div 8 =$

(18) $73 \div 9 =$

(19) $74 \div 8 =$

(20) $74 \div 9 =$

(21) $75 \div 8 =$

(22) $75 \div 9 =$

(23) $76 \div 8 =$

(24) $76 \div 9 =$

(25) $77 \div 8 =$

2 Divide.

2 points per question

(1) 75 ÷ 9 =

(2) 76 ÷ 8 =

(3) 76 ÷ 9 =

(4) 77 ÷ 8 =

(5) 77 ÷ 9 =

(6) 78 ÷ 8 =

(7) 78 ÷ 9 =

(8) 79 ÷ 8 =

(9) 79 ÷ 9 =

(10) 80 ÷ 8 =

(11) 80 ÷ 9 =

(12) 60 ÷ 10 =

(13) 70 ÷ 10 =

(14) 80 ÷ 10 =

(15) 81 ÷ 9 =

(16) 82 ÷ 9 =

(17) 84 ÷ 9 =

(18) 85 ÷ 9 =

(19) 86 ÷ 9 =

(20) 87 ÷ 9 =

(21) 88 ÷ 9 =

(22) 89 ÷ 9 =

(23) 90 ÷ 9 =

(24) 80 ÷ 10 =

(25) 90 ÷ 10 =

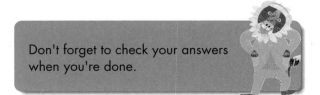

Don't forget to check your answers when you're done.

31 Division with Remainders

Level ★★

Date / /

Name

Score /100

1 Divide.

2 points per question

(1) $21 \div 4 =$

(2) $22 \div 5 =$

(3) $23 \div 6 =$

(4) $24 \div 7 =$

(5) $25 \div 8 =$

(6) $26 \div 9 =$

(7) $27 \div 3 =$

(8) $28 \div 4 =$

(9) $29 \div 5 =$

(10) $30 \div 3 =$

(11) $31 \div 7 =$

(12) $32 \div 8 =$

(13) $33 \div 9 =$

(14) $34 \div 4 =$

(15) $35 \div 5 =$

(16) $36 \div 6 =$

(17) $37 \div 7 =$

(18) $38 \div 8 =$

(19) $39 \div 9 =$

(20) $40 \div 10 =$

(21) $41 \div 5 =$

(22) $42 \div 6 =$

(23) $43 \div 7 =$

(24) $44 \div 8 =$

(25) $45 \div 9 =$

② Divide.

2 points per question

(1) $22 \div 3 =$

(2) $33 \div 4 =$

(3) $34 \div 5 =$

(4) $35 \div 4 =$

(5) $37 \div 8 =$

(6) $38 \div 9 =$

(7) $41 \div 7 =$

(8) $42 \div 8 =$

(9) $43 \div 9 =$

(10) $44 \div 6 =$

(11) $45 \div 7 =$

(12) $46 \div 8 =$

(13) $47 \div 9 =$

(14) $49 \div 7 =$

(15) $50 \div 10 =$

(16) $51 \div 8 =$

(17) $52 \div 9 =$

(18) $53 \div 7 =$

(19) $54 \div 8 =$

(20) $56 \div 6 =$

(21) $58 \div 8 =$

(22) $58 \div 9 =$

(23) $59 \div 8 =$

(24) $59 \div 9 =$

(25) $60 \div 6 =$

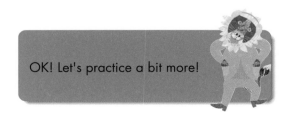

OK! Let's practice a bit more!

Division with Remainders

Level ★★

1 Divide.

2 points per question

(1) $40 \div 4 =$

(2) $40 \div 5 =$

(3) $41 \div 6 =$

(4) $42 \div 7 =$

(5) $43 \div 8 =$

(6) $44 \div 9 =$

(7) $45 \div 5 =$

(8) $45 \div 6 =$

(9) $47 \div 5 =$

(10) $48 \div 6 =$

(11) $49 \div 7 =$

(12) $60 \div 6 =$

(13) $60 \div 10 =$

(14) $67 \div 7 =$

(15) $68 \div 8 =$

(16) $69 \div 7 =$

(17) $69 \div 9 =$

(18) $70 \div 7 =$

(19) $70 \div 9 =$

(20) $71 \div 8 =$

(21) $72 \div 8 =$

(22) $73 \div 9 =$

(23) $74 \div 8 =$

(24) $75 \div 9 =$

(25) $83 \div 9 =$

2 Divide.

2 points per question

(1) $51 \div 7 =$

(2) $52 \div 6 =$

(3) $53 \div 9 =$

(4) $54 \div 8 =$

(5) $56 \div 7 =$

(6) $57 \div 8 =$

(7) $58 \div 9 =$

(8) $61 \div 9 =$

(9) $62 \div 8 =$

(10) $65 \div 7 =$

(11) $67 \div 9 =$

(12) $68 \div 8 =$

(13) $69 \div 9 =$

(14) $70 \div 8 =$

(15) $70 \div 9 =$

(16) $70 \div 10 =$

(17) $71 \div 9 =$

(18) $72 \div 8 =$

(19) $73 \div 9 =$

(20) $74 \div 8 =$

(21) $75 \div 9 =$

(22) $78 \div 8 =$

(23) $81 \div 9 =$

(24) $83 \div 9 =$

(25) $86 \div 9 =$

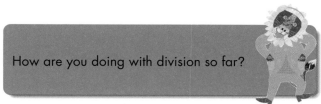

How are you doing with division so far?

Division with Remainders

Date   /   /

Name

Score

/100

1 Divide.

2 points per question

(1) $15 \div 2 =$

(2) $18 \div 5 =$

(3) $27 \div 4 =$

(4) $16 \div 3 =$

(5) $32 \div 7 =$

(6) $24 \div 9 =$

(7) $17 \div 3 =$

(8) $41 \div 8 =$

(9) $36 \div 5 =$

(10) $40 \div 4 =$

(11) $28 \div 6 =$

(12) $14 \div 3 =$

(13) $35 \div 9 =$

(14) $20 \div 2 =$

(15) $44 \div 9 =$

(16) $16 \div 2 =$

(17) $30 \div 7 =$

(18) $34 \div 6 =$

(19) $18 \div 8 =$

(20) $12 \div 5 =$

(21) $25 \div 4 =$

(22) $45 \div 6 =$

(23) $33 \div 9 =$

(24) $30 \div 10 =$

(25) $42 \div 8 =$

② Divide.

2 points per question

(1) $40 \div 7 =$

(2) $52 \div 6 =$

(3) $71 \div 9 =$

(4) $48 \div 5 =$

(5) $63 \div 7 =$

(6) $55 \div 8 =$

(7) $32 \div 6 =$

(8) $49 \div 5 =$

(9) $75 \div 8 =$

(10) $51 \div 7 =$

(11) $60 \div 6 =$

(12) $82 \div 9 =$

(13) $43 \div 6 =$

(14) $54 \div 8 =$

(15) $60 \div 7 =$

(16) $47 \div 6 =$

(17) $73 \div 9 =$

(18) $68 \div 7 =$

(19) $35 \div 5 =$

(20) $52 \div 8 =$

(21) $70 \div 10 =$

(22) $85 \div 9 =$

(23) $62 \div 7 =$

(24) $46 \div 6 =$

(25) $58 \div 8 =$

Great job! Now let's try something new!

1 Divide.

4 points

$10 \div 2 = \boxed{}$ → vertical form → $2\overline{)10}$ $\boxed{}$ 👉 Write the answer here.

2 Divide.

2 points per question

(1) $2\overline{)12}$ $\boxed{}$

(2) $2\overline{)16}$

(3) $2\overline{)18}$

(4) $3\overline{)12}$

(5) $3\overline{)15}$

(6) $3\overline{)18}$

(7) $3\overline{)27}$

(8) $4\overline{)12}$

(9) $4\overline{)20}$

(10) $4\overline{)28}$

(11) $4\overline{)36}$

(12) $5\overline{)15}$

(13) $5\overline{)20}$

(14) $5\overline{)35}$

(15) $5\overline{)40}$

(16) $6\overline{)12}$

(17) $6\overline{)18}$

(18) $6\overline{)30}$

3 Divide.

3 points per question

(1) 7)14

(2) 7)28

(3) 7)35

(4) 8)24

(5) 8)40

(6) 9)18

(7) 9)36

(8) 2)12

(9) 3)12

(10) 6)12

(11) 3)24

(12) 4)24

(13) 6)24

(14) 8)24

(15) 4)36

(16) 6)36

(17) 9)36

(18) 6)48

(19) 8)48

(20) 9)45

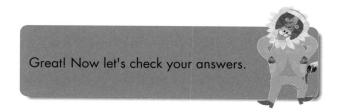

Great! Now let's check your answers.

Vertical Form Division

Level ★★★

Date / /

Name

Score /100

1 **Divide.**

4 points

$14 \div 3 = \boxed{} R \boxed{}$ → vertical form → $3\overline{)14}$ $\boxed{} R \boxed{}$

2 **Divide.**

2 points per question

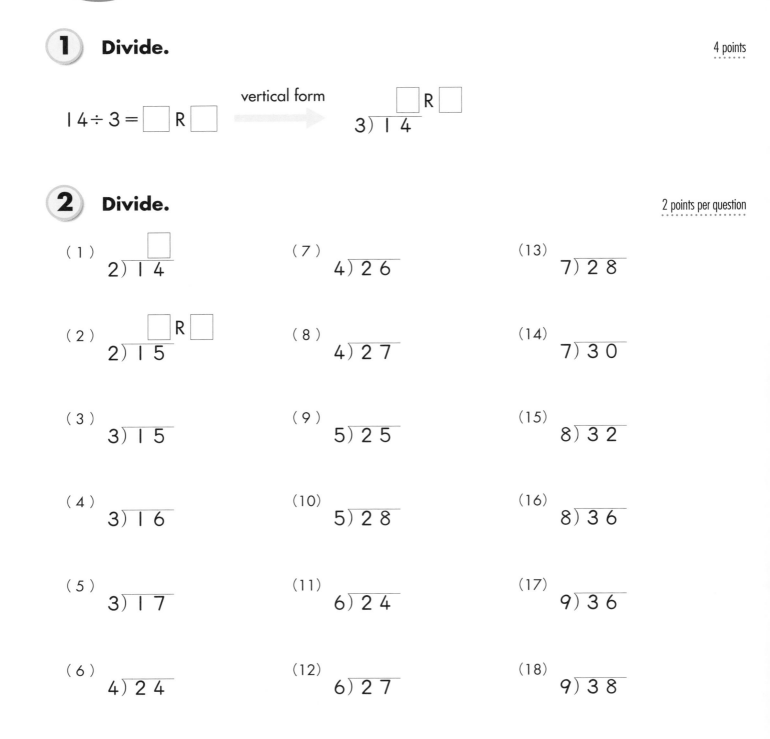

(1) $2\overline{)14}$ $\boxed{}$

(2) $2\overline{)15}$ $\boxed{} R \boxed{}$

(3) $3\overline{)15}$

(4) $3\overline{)16}$

(5) $3\overline{)17}$

(6) $4\overline{)24}$

(7) $4\overline{)26}$

(8) $4\overline{)27}$

(9) $5\overline{)25}$

(10) $5\overline{)28}$

(11) $6\overline{)24}$

(12) $6\overline{)27}$

(13) $7\overline{)28}$

(14) $7\overline{)30}$

(15) $8\overline{)32}$

(16) $8\overline{)36}$

(17) $9\overline{)36}$

(18) $9\overline{)38}$

3 Divide.

(1)
2)16

(2)
2)17

(3)
3)18

(4)
3)19

(5)
3)20

(6)
4)20

(7)
4)22

(8)
4)23

(9)
5)30

(10)
5)31

(11)
5)34

(12)
6)36

(13)
6)37

(14)
6)40

(15)
7)42

(16)
7)45

(17)
8)48

(18)
8)50

(19)
9)54

(20)
9)57

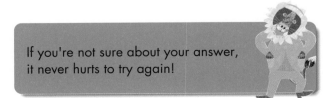

If you're not sure about your answer, it never hurts to try again!

36

Vertical Form Division

Date   /   /

Name

1 Divide.

2 points per question

(1)
$$2 \overline{)16}$$

(2)
$$3 \overline{)16}$$

(3)
$$4 \overline{)16}$$

(4)
$$5 \overline{)16}$$

(5)
$$3 \overline{)20}$$

(6)
$$4 \overline{)20}$$

(7)
$$6 \overline{)20}$$

(8)
$$3 \overline{)25}$$

(9)
$$4 \overline{)25}$$

(10)
$$5 \overline{)25}$$

(11)
$$3 \overline{)27}$$

(12)
$$4 \overline{)27}$$

(13)
$$4 \overline{)28}$$

(14)
$$5 \overline{)28}$$

(15)
$$6 \overline{)28}$$

(16)
$$4 \overline{)32}$$

(17)
$$5 \overline{)32}$$

(18)
$$6 \overline{)32}$$

(19)
$$7 \overline{)32}$$

(20)
$$8 \overline{)32}$$

2 Divide.

3 points per question

(1) 4)36

(2) 5)36

(3) 6)36

(4) 7)36

(5) 8)36

(6) 5)40

(7) 6)40

(8) 7)40

(9) 8)40

(10) 9)40

(11) 6)48

(12) 7)48

(13) 8)48

(14) 9)48

(15) 6)56

(16) 7)56

(17) 8)56

(18) 9)56

(19) 7)63

(20) 8)63

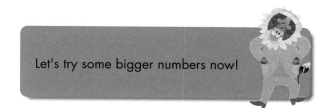

Let's try some bigger numbers now!

Vertical Form Division

Level ★★★

Date   /   /

Name

Score

/100

1 **Divide.**

2 points per question

(1)
2) 2 4

(8)
2) 3 0

(15)
3) 4 2

(2)
2) 2 8

(9)
2) 3 2

(16)
3) 4 8

(3)
2) 4 2

(10)
2) 3 4

(17)
3) 5 4

(4)
3) 3 6

(11)
2) 3 6

(18)
3) 7 2

(5)
3) 3 3

(12)
2) 5 0

(19)
3) 8 1

(6)
3) 6 0

(13)
2) 5 2

(20)
3) 9 9

(7)
3) 9 3

(14)
2) 5 6

2 Divide.

(1) 3)24

(2) 3)36

(3) 3)51

(4) 4)44

(5) 4)48

(6) 4)52

(7) 4)72

(8) 5)15

(9) 5)75

(10) 5)60

(11) 5)80

(12) 6)30

(13) 6)66

(14) 6)72

(15) 6)84

(16) 6)90

(17) 2)52

(18) 3)51

(19) 4)52

(20) 2)54

Great work! Now let's check your score.

Vertical Form Division

Level ★★★

Date / /

Name

Score /100

1 Divide.

2 points per question

(1)

2)56

(2)

4)56

(3)

7)56

(4)

8)56

(5)

3)57

(6)

2)58

(7)

2)60

(8)

3)60

(9)

4)60

(10)

5)60

(11)

2)64

(12)

4)64

(13)

8)64

(14)

5)65

(15)

2)66

(16)

6)66

(17)

2)68

(18)

4)68

(19)

2)70

(20)

5)70

2 Divide.

3 points per question

(1) 2)78

(2) 3)78

(3) 6)78

(4) 3)81

(5) 9)81

(6) 3)84

(7) 6)84

(8) 7)84

(9) 2)90

(10) 3)90

(11) 5)90

(12) 6)90

(13) 9)90

(14) 2)92

(15) 4)92

(16) 3)96

(17) 4)96

(18) 8)96

(19) 3)99

(20) 9)99

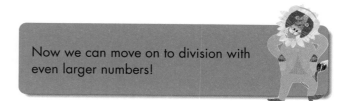

Now we can move on to division with even larger numbers!

Division of Large Numbers

Date / /

Name

Score /100

1 Divide.

2 points per question

(1) $60 \div 2 = 30$

(2) $60 \div 3 =$

(3) $80 \div 2 =$

(4) $80 \div 4 =$

(5) $90 \div 3 =$

(6) $100 \div 5 =$

(7) $120 \div 3 =$

(8) $120 \div 6 =$

(9) $140 \div 2 =$

(10) $140 \div 7 =$

(11) $150 \div 3 =$

(12) $150 \div 5 =$

(13) $160 \div 2 =$

(14) $160 \div 4 =$

(15) $160 \div 8 =$

(16) $180 \div 2 =$

(17) $180 \div 3 =$

(18) $180 \div 9 =$

(19) $200 \div 4 =$

(20) $200 \div 5 =$

2 Divide.

3 points per question

(1) $210 \div 3 =$

(2) $210 \div 7 =$

(3) $240 \div 3 =$

(4) $240 \div 8 =$

(5) $270 \div 3 =$

(6) $280 \div 7 =$

(7) $300 \div 6 =$

(8) $320 \div 4 =$

(9) $320 \div 8 =$

(10) $350 \div 5 =$

(11) $360 \div 4 =$

(12) $360 \div 6 =$

(13) $400 \div 8 =$

(14) $420 \div 6 =$

(15) $480 \div 6 =$

(16) $490 \div 7 =$

(17) $540 \div 9 =$

(18) $560 \div 7 =$

(19) $630 \div 9 =$

(20) $720 \div 8 =$

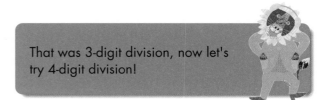

That was 3-digit division, now let's try 4-digit division!

40

Date   /   /

Name

Score

/100

1 Divide.

2 points per question

(1) $600 \div 2 = 300$

(2) $600 \div 3 =$

(3) $800 \div 2 =$

(4) $800 \div 4 =$

(5) $900 \div 3 =$

(6) $1000 \div 2 =$

(7) $1000 \div 5 =$

(8) $1200 \div 3 =$

(9) $1200 \div 4 =$

(10) $1400 \div 2 =$

(11) $1400 \div 7 =$

(12) $1500 \div 3 =$

(13) $1500 \div 5 =$

(14) $1600 \div 2 =$

(15) $1600 \div 4 =$

(16) $1600 \div 8 =$

(17) $1800 \div 2 =$

(18) $1800 \div 3 =$

(19) $1800 \div 6 =$

(20) $1800 \div 9 =$

3 points per question

(1) 2000÷4 =500

(2) 2000÷5 =

(3) 2100÷3 =

(4) 2400÷4 =

(5) 2400÷6 =

(6) 2700÷3 =

(7) 2700÷9 =

(8) 2800÷7 =

(9) 3000÷5 =

(10) 3200÷4 =

(11) 3500÷7 =

(12) 3600÷4 =

(13) 3600÷6 =

(14) 4000÷8 =

(15) 4200÷6 =

(16) 4500÷5 =

(17) 4800÷8 =

(18) 5400÷9 =

(19) 6300÷7 =

(20) 7200÷8 =

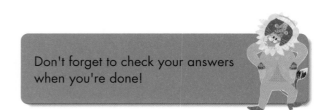

Don't forget to check your answers when you're done!

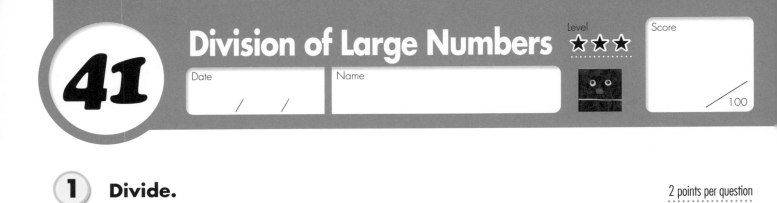

Division of Large Numbers

Level ★★★

Date   /   /

Name

Score

/100

1 Divide.

2 points per question

(1) $60 \div 20 = 3$

(2) $60 \div 30 =$

(3) $80 \div 20 = \boxed{}$

(4) $80 \div 30 = \boxed{2}$ R $\boxed{20}$

(5) $90 \div 20 =$

(6) $90 \div 30 =$

(7) $100 \div 20 =$

(8) $100 \div 30 =$

(9) $100 \div 40 =$

(10) $120 \div 40 =$

(11) $120 \div 50 =$

(12) $150 \div 30 =$

(13) $150 \div 40 =$

(14) $160 \div 50 =$

(15) $170 \div 60 =$

(16) $180 \div 30 =$

(17) $180 \div 40 =$

(18) $200 \div 50 =$

(19) $200 \div 60 =$

(20) $200 \div 70 =$

② Divide.

(1) 240÷40=

(2) 240÷50=

(3) 280÷70=

(4) 280÷80=

(5) 320÷80=

(6) 320÷90=

(7) 360÷50=

(8) 360÷60=

(9) 400÷70=

(10) 420÷60=

(11) 450÷60=

(12) 450÷80=

(13) 450÷90=

(14) 480÷90=

(15) 500÷60=

(16) 540÷60=

(17) 540÷70=

(18) 600÷70=

(19) 600÷80=

(20) 630÷80=

Have you mastered your division?

1 Divide.

2 points per question

(1) $600 \div 200 = 3$

(2) $600 \div 300 =$

(3) $600 \div 100 =$

(4) $800 \div 200 =$

(5) $800 \div 400 =$

(6) $1000 \div 200 =$

(7) $1000 \div 500 =$

(8) $1200 \div 300 =$

(9) $1200 \div 400 =$

(10) $1200 \div 600 =$

(11) $1400 \div 700 =$

(12) $1500 \div 300 =$

(13) $1500 \div 500 =$

(14) $1600 \div 200 =$

(15) $1600 \div 400 =$

(16) $1800 \div 200 =$

(17) $1800 \div 600 =$

(18) $1800 \div 900 =$

(19) $2000 \div 400 =$

(20) $2000 \div 500 =$

② Divide.

3 points per question

(1) $2100 \div 300 =$

(2) $2400 \div 300 =$

(3) $2400 \div 400 =$

(4) $2700 \div 300 =$

(5) $2800 \div 700 =$

(6) $3000 \div 500 =$

(7) $3200 \div 400 =$

(8) $3200 \div 800 =$

(9) $3500 \div 700 =$

(10) $3600 \div 400 =$

(11) $3600 \div 900 =$

(12) $4000 \div 800 =$

(13) $4200 \div 700 =$

(14) $4500 \div 900 =$

(15) $4800 \div 800 =$

(16) $5400 \div 600 =$

(17) $5600 \div 700 =$

(18) $6300 \div 700 =$

(19) $6400 \div 800 =$

(20) $7200 \div 900 =$

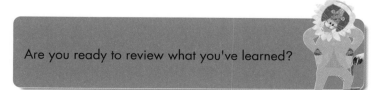

Are you ready to review what you've learned?

43 **Review**

Date / /

Name

Level ★★★

Score

/100

1 Divide.

1 point per question

(1) $18 \div 2 =$

(2) $14 \div 7 =$

(3) $20 \div 4 =$

(4) $24 \div 8 =$

(5) $21 \div 3 =$

(6) $25 \div 5 =$

(7) $36 \div 6 =$

(8) $32 \div 4 =$

(9) $36 \div 9 =$

(10) $42 \div 6 =$

(11) $48 \div 8 =$

(12) $54 \div 9 =$

(13) $49 \div 7 =$

(14) $64 \div 8 =$

(15) $63 \div 9 =$

(16) $72 \div 8 =$

2 Divide.

1 point per question

(1) $12 \div 4 =$

(2) $12 \div 5 =$

(3) $18 \div 3 =$

(4) $18 \div 4 =$

(5) $24 \div 6 =$

(6) $24 \div 7 =$

(7) $35 \div 6 =$

(8) $35 \div 7 =$

(9) $42 \div 7 =$

(10) $42 \div 8 =$

(11) $54 \div 8 =$

(12) $54 \div 9 =$

3 Divide.

2 points per question

(1) $32 \div 5 =$

(2) $44 \div 6 =$

(3) $17 \div 8 =$

(4) $54 \div 7 =$

(5) $48 \div 6 =$

(6) $64 \div 9 =$

(7) $70 \div 10 =$

(8) $25 \div 4 =$

(9) $52 \div 6 =$

(10) $43 \div 8 =$

(11) $63 \div 7 =$

(12) $35 \div 4 =$

(13) $80 \div 9 =$

(14) $56 \div 6 =$

(15) $30 \div 3 =$

(16) $16 \div 7 =$

(17) $65 \div 9 =$

(18) $28 \div 4 =$

(19) $46 \div 5 =$

(20) $80 \div 8 =$

(21) $34 \div 6 =$

(22) $55 \div 7 =$

(23) $42 \div 6 =$

(24) $48 \div 5 =$

(25) $64 \div 8 =$

(26) $78 \div 9 =$

(27) $26 \div 3 =$

(28) $62 \div 7 =$

(29) $86 \div 9 =$

(30) $54 \div 8 =$

4 Divide.

2 points per question

(1) $560 \div 8 =$

(2) $720 \div 9 =$

(3) $4800 \div 600 =$

(4) $700 \div 80 =$

(5) $100 \div 30 =$

(6) $170 \div 60 =$

Congratulations! You are ready for *Grade 4 Multiplication*!

1 Multiplication Review   pp 2, 3

1
(1) 10 (15) 9 (29) 16
(2) 15 (16) 12 (30) 18
(3) 20 (17) 2 (31) 0
(4) 25 (18) 4 (32) 32
(5) 12 (19) 6 (33) 36
(6) 18 (20) 8 (34) 0
(7) 24 (21) 5 (35) 24
(8) 30 (22) 10 (36) 27
(9) 14 (23) 15 (37) 0
(10) 21 (24) 20 (38) 40
(11) 28 (25) 4 (39) 45
(12) 35 (26) 8 (40) 0
(13) 3 (27) 12
(14) 6 (28) 16

2
(1) 24 (11) 0 (21) 32
(2) 6 (12) 24 (22) 10
(3) 40 (13) 16 (23) 30
(4) 15 (14) 12 (24) 27
(5) 12 (15) 5 (25) 4
(6) 20 (16) 9 (26) 16
(7) 14 (17) 18 (27) 21
(8) 3 (18) 8 (28) 15
(9) 45 (19) 35 (29) 4
(10) 8 (20) 0 (30) 36

2 Multiplication Review   pp 4, 5

1
(1) 30 (15) 21 (29) 48
(2) 35 (16) 28 (30) 54
(3) 40 (17) 6 (31) 0
(4) 45 (18) 12 (32) 64
(5) 36 (19) 18 (33) 72
(6) 42 (20) 24 (34) 0
(7) 48 (21) 9 (35) 56
(8) 54 (22) 18 (36) 63
(9) 42 (23) 27 (37) 0
(10) 49 (24) 36 (38) 72
(11) 56 (25) 8 (39) 81
(12) 63 (26) 16 (40) 0
(13) 7 (27) 24
(14) 14 (28) 32

2
(1) 48 (11) 0 (21) 64
(2) 18 (12) 56 (22) 30
(3) 72 (13) 32 (23) 54
(4) 35 (14) 36 (24) 63
(5) 24 (15) 9 (25) 8
(6) 36 (16) 21 (26) 48
(7) 42 (17) 54 (27) 49
(8) 7 (18) 16 (28) 27
(9) 81 (19) 63 (29) 12
(10) 24 (20) 0 (30) 72

3 Multiplication Review   pp 6, 7

1
(1) 24 (18) 30 (35) 14
(2) 20 (19) 24 (36) 64
(3) 16 (20) 45 (37) 56
(4) 63 (21) 40 (38) 48
(5) 56 (22) 35 (39) 18
(6) 49 (23) 27 (40) 15
(7) 12 (24) 18 (41) 12
(8) 10 (25) 9 (42) 54
(9) 8 (26) 0 (43) 48
(10) 24 (27) 36 (44) 42
(11) 16 (28) 32 (45) 30
(12) 8 (29) 28 (46) 20
(13) 0 (30) 35 (47) 10
(14) 27 (31) 21 (48) 45
(15) 24 (32) 7 (49) 63
(16) 21 (33) 18 (50) 81
(17) 36 (34) 16

2
(1) 10 (18) 3 (35) 28
(2) 15 (19) 35 (36) 45
(3) 56 (20) 27 (37) 4
(4) 9 (21) 16 (38) 48
(5) 28 (22) 42 (39) 24
(6) 18 (23) 16 (40) 12
(7) 48 (24) 18 (41) 63
(8) 8 (25) 54 (42) 24
(9) 72 (26) 21 (43) 20
(10) 9 (27) 0 (44) 42
(11) 25 (28) 21 (45) 6
(12) 49 (29) 10 (46) 40
(13) 4 (30) 64 (47) 36
(14) 32 (31) 24 (48) 12
(15) 54 (32) 36 (49) 35
(16) 24 (33) 30 (50) 81
(17) 40 (34) 6

4 Multiplication Review   pp 8, 9

1
(1) 3 (6) 1
(2) 6 (7) 1
(3) 8 (8) 0
(4) 6 (9) 0
(5) 3 (10) 0

2
(1) 2 (11) 5 (21) 7
(2) 2 (12) 5 (22) 0
(3) 3 (13) 0 (23) 9
(4) 3 (14) 0 (24) 0
(5) 0 (15) 0 (25) 8
(6) 0 (16) 0 (26) 0
(7) 0 (17) 6 (27) 1
(8) 0 (18) 6 (28) 0
(9) 4 (19) 0 (29) 0
(10) 4 (20) 0 (30) 0

3
(1) 18 (21) 27 (41) 0
(2) 5 (22) 12 (42) 56
(3) 32 (23) 0 (43) 12
(4) 42 (24) 10 (44) 9
(5) 0 (25) 48 (45) 36
(6) 32 (26) 4 (46) 14
(7) 27 (27) 12 (47) 0
(8) 7 (28) 35 (48) 45
(9) 45 (29) 0 (49) 30
(10) 8 (30) 40 (50) 0
(11) 0 (31) 21 (51) 16
(12) 25 (32) 6 (52) 56
(13) 42 (33) 72 (53) 0
(14) 3 (34) 4 (54) 72
(15) 24 (35) 0 (55) 18
(16) 63 (36) 40 (56) 8
(17) 0 (37) 0 (57) 81
(18) 64 (38) 2 (58) 6
(19) 15 (39) 28 (59) 0
(20) 1 (40) 21 (60) 35

5 Multiplication Review   pp 10, 11

1

(1) 18	(18) 9	(35) 70
(2) 20	(19) 10	(36) 70
(3) 45	(20) 10	(37) 80
(4) 50	(21) 20	(38) 40
(5) 36	(22) 50	(39) 20
(6) 40	(23) 40	(40) 60
(7) 54	(24) 60	(41) 60
(8) 60	(25) 80	(42) 50
(9) 72	(26) 30	(43) 40
(10) 80	(27) 70	(44) 10
(11) 27	(28) 90	(45) 0
(12) 30	(29) 100	(46) 90
(13) 63	(30) 20	(47) 80
(14) 70	(31) 10	(48) 100
(15) 81	(32) 0	(49) 20
(16) 90	(33) 30	(50) 10
(17) 100	(34) 30	

2

(1) 27	(18) 30	(35) 56
(2) 30	(19) 80	(36) 45
(3) 28	(20) 63	(37) 90
(4) 50	(21) 14	(38) 21
(5) 0	(22) 40	(39) 0
(6) 48	(23) 70	(40) 81
(7) 70	(24) 54	(41) 8
(8) 72	(25) 60	(42) 100
(9) 20	(26) 32	(43) 64
(10) 80	(27) 0	(44) 90
(11) 0	(28) 20	(45) 40
(12) 15	(29) 18	(46) 0
(13) 10	(30) 50	(47) 56
(14) 42	(31) 10	(48) 54
(15) 60	(32) 0	(49) 70
(16) 90	(33) 42	(50) 18
(17) 32	(34) 100	

6 Multiplication Review   pp 12, 13

1

(1) 21	(21) 28	(41) 49
(2) 20	(22) 0	(42) 8
(3) 48	(23) 18	(43) 42
(4) 3	(24) 1	(44) 5
(5) 10	(25) 45	(45) 15
(6) 54	(26) 63	(46) 72
(7) 0	(27) 0	(47) 0
(8) 8	(28) 12	(48) 4
(9) 8	(29) 32	(49) 40
(10) 18	(30) 24	(50) 0
(11) 63	(31) 0	(51) 42
(12) 4	(32) 28	(52) 36
(13) 0	(33) 30	(53) 12
(14) 8	(34) 2	(54) 7
(15) 25	(35) 30	(55) 40
(16) 18	(36) 27	(56) 9
(17) 0	(37) 0	(57) 0
(18) 14	(38) 10	(58) 2
(19) 48	(39) 64	(59) 24
(20) 6	(40) 12	(60) 27

2

(1) 35	(15) 30	(29) 0
(2) 12	(16) 45	(30) 70
(3) 54	(17) 0	(31) 14
(4) 4	(18) 6	(32) 32
(5) 35	(19) 72	(33) 100
(6) 36	(20) 40	(34) 6
(7) 0	(21) 56	(35) 5
(8) 20	(22) 50	(36) 81
(9) 56	(23) 36	(37) 0
(10) 15	(24) 0	(38) 90
(11) 7	(25) 20	(39) 16
(12) 24	(26) 0	(40) 80
(13) 60	(27) 0	
(14) 9	(28) 18	

7 Inverse Multiplication   pp 14, 15

1

(1) 3	(15) 7	(29) 9
(2) 4	(16) 3	(30) 7
(3) 7	(17) 6	(31) 9
(4) 8	(18) 8	(32) 2
(5) 2	(19) 8	(33) 8
(6) 5	(20) 0	(34) 5
(7) 9	(21) 7	(35) 7
(8) 0	(22) 9	(36) 6
(9) 6	(23) 6	(37) 9
(10) 1	(24) 9	(38) 7
(11) 5	(25) 5	(39) 4
(12) 8	(26) 7	(40) 9
(13) 6	(27) 8	
(14) 7	(28) 1	

2

(1) 2	(11) 7	(21) 5
(2) 3	(12) 3	(22) 8
(3) 9	(13) 5	(23) 2
(4) 7	(14) 2	(24) 5
(5) 3	(15) 9	(25) 9
(6) 4	(16) 3	(26) 1
(7) 8	(17) 9	(27) 4
(8) 6	(18) 7	(28) 8
(9) 4	(19) 4	(29) 3
(10) 2	(20) 8	(30) 6

8 Division   pp 16, 17

1

(1) $2 \times \boxed{4} = 8$	$8 \div 2 = \boxed{4}$
(2) $2 \times \boxed{6} = 12$	$12 \div 2 = \boxed{6}$
(3) $3 \times \boxed{5} = 15$	$15 \div 3 = \boxed{5}$
(4) $3 \times \boxed{6} = 18$	$18 \div 3 = \boxed{6}$
(5) $4 \times \boxed{6} = 24$	$24 \div 4 = \boxed{6}$
(6) $4 \times \boxed{9} = 36$	$36 \div 4 = \boxed{9}$
(7) $5 \times \boxed{5} = 25$	$25 \div 5 = \boxed{5}$
(8) $5 \times \boxed{8} = 40$	$40 \div 5 = \boxed{8}$
(9) $6 \times \boxed{7} = 42$	$42 \div 6 = \boxed{7}$
(10) $7 \times \boxed{3} = 21$	$21 \div 7 = \boxed{3}$
(11) $8 \times \boxed{6} = 48$	$48 \div 8 = \boxed{6}$
(12) $9 \times \boxed{7} = 63$	$63 \div 9 = \boxed{7}$
(13) $10 \times \boxed{6} = 60$	$60 \div 10 = \boxed{6}$

2

(1) $\boxed{2} \times 2 = 4$	$4 \div 2 = \boxed{2}$
(2) $\boxed{5} \times 2 = 10$	$10 \div 2 = \boxed{5}$
(3) $\boxed{7} \times 3 = 21$	$21 \div 3 = \boxed{7}$
(4) $\boxed{9} \times 3 = 27$	$27 \div 3 = \boxed{9}$
(5) $\boxed{4} \times 4 = 16$	$16 \div 4 = \boxed{4}$
(6) $\boxed{8} \times 4 = 32$	$32 \div 4 = \boxed{8}$
(7) $\boxed{6} \times 5 = 30$	$30 \div 5 = \boxed{6}$
(8) $\boxed{8} \times 6 = 48$	$48 \div 6 = \boxed{8}$
(9) $\boxed{5} \times 7 = 35$	$35 \div 7 = \boxed{5}$
(10) $\boxed{4} \times 8 = 32$	$32 \div 8 = \boxed{4}$
(11) $\boxed{8} \times 9 = 72$	$72 \div 9 = \boxed{8}$
(12) $\boxed{8} \times 10 = 80$	$80 \div 10 = \boxed{8}$

Advice

If you scored over 85 on this section, review your mistakes and move on to the next section.

If you scored between 75 and 84 on this section, review the beginning of this book before moving on.

If you scored less than 74 on this section, it might be a good idea to go back to our "Grade 3 Multiplication" book and do an extended review of multiplication.

9 Division
pp 18, 19

1

(1) 4	(10) 0	(19) 2
(2) 6	(11) 2	(20) 6
(3) 8	(12) 5	(21) 4
(4) 3	(13) 7	(22) 7
(5) 2	(14) 1	(23) 0
(6) 1	(15) 8	(24) 9
(7) 5	(16) 6	(25) 5
(8) 9	(17) 0	
(9) 7	(18) 9	

2

(1) 3	(10) 6	(19) 5
(2) 2	(11) 0	(20) 4
(3) 7	(12) 3	(21) 8
(4) 4	(13) 8	(22) 0
(5) 1	(14) 7	(23) 6
(6) 0	(15) 9	(24) 1
(7) 8	(16) 4	(25) 9
(8) 2	(17) 3	
(9) 5	(18) 7	

10 Division
pp 20, 21

1

(1) 4	(10) 2	(19) 9
(2) 8	(11) 6	(20) 6
(3) 2	(12) 7	(21) 3
(4) 1	(13) 9	(22) 8
(5) 9	(14) 5	(23) 1
(6) 5	(15) 2	(24) 4
(7) 3	(16) 1	(25) 7
(8) 5	(17) 8	
(9) 8	(18) 7	

2

(1) 3	(10) 5	(19) 9
(2) 8	(11) 9	(20) 2
(3) 7	(12) 3	(21) 5
(4) 2	(13) 7	(22) 3
(5) 5	(14) 4	(23) 1
(6) 1	(15) 2	(24) 4
(7) 1	(16) 7	(25) 6
(8) 6	(17) 1	
(9) 2	(18) 5	

11 Division
pp 22, 23

1

(1) 3	(10) 8	(19) 2
(2) 7	(11) 1	(20) 1
(3) 2	(12) 6	(21) 6
(4) 8	(13) 4	(22) 3
(5) 4	(14) 2	(23) 9
(6) 5	(15) 4	(24) 4
(7) 2	(16) 7	(25) 8
(8) 5	(17) 9	
(9) 3	(18) 5	

2

(1) 5	(10) 2	(19) 2
(2) 9	(11) 5	(20) 6
(3) 3	(12) 8	(21) 2
(4) 5	(13) 9	(22) 9
(5) 8	(14) 4	(23) 2
(6) 3	(15) 1	(24) 5
(7) 1	(16) 7	(25) 7
(8) 9	(17) 3	
(9) 3	(18) 9	

12 Division
pp 24, 25

1

(1) 3	(10) 4	(19) 3
(2) 3	(11) 3	(20) 5
(3) 2	(12) 3	(21) 6
(4) 2	(13) 3	(22) 4
(5) 1	(14) 5	(23) 5
(6) 2	(15) 5	(24) 5
(7) 2	(16) 4	(25) 5
(8) 2	(17) 3	
(9) 4	(18) 4	

2

(1) 5	(10) 7	(19) 8
(2) 6	(11) 5	(20) 8
(3) 7	(12) 7	(21) 9
(4) 6	(13) 7	(22) 9
(5) 6	(14) 6	(23) 9
(6) 6	(15) 7	(24) 9
(7) 7	(16) 6	(25) 9
(8) 7	(17) 8	
(9) 6	(18) 9	

13 Division
pp 26, 27

1

(1) 4	(10) 4	(19) 5
(2) 3	(11) 9	(20) 7
(3) 4	(12) 6	(21) 6
(4) 8	(13) 6	(22) 7
(5) 6	(14) 6	(23) 7
(6) 5	(15) 4	(24) 6
(7) 4	(16) 4	(25) 6
(8) 4	(17) 5	
(9) 4	(18) 5	

2

(1) 6	(10) 8	(19) 9
(2) 7	(11) 9	(20) 7
(3) 8	(12) 8	(21) 7
(4) 9	(13) 8	(22) 9
(5) 4	(14) 6	(23) 8
(6) 7	(15) 7	(24) 9
(7) 4	(16) 4	(25) 9
(8) 3	(17) 5	
(9) 5	(18) 9	

14 Division
pp 28, 29

1

(1) 2	(10) 1	(19) 4
(2) 1	(11) 3	(20) 2
(3) 2	(12) 3	(21) 1
(4) 0	(13) 2	(22) 6
(5) 7	(14) 1	(23) 1
(6) 3	(15) 7	(24) 0
(7) 1	(16) 0	(25) 8
(8) 5	(17) 4	
(9) 4	(18) 1	

2

(1) 8	(10) 4	(19) 6
(2) 1	(11) 0	(20) 9
(3) 2	(12) 4	(21) 5
(4) 5	(13) 5	(22) 5
(5) 3	(14) 3	(23) 1
(6) 0	(15) 1	(24) 8
(7) 3	(16) 0	(25) 8
(8) 8	(17) 6	
(9) 1	(18) 1	

15 Division
pp 30, 31

1

(1) 4	(10) 9	(19) 8
(2) 5	(11) 3	(20) 7
(3) 2	(12) 3	(21) 4
(4) 4	(13) 5	(22) 4
(5) 6	(14) 6	(23) 8
(6) 6	(15) 7	(24) 9
(7) 3	(16) 5	(25) 5
(8) 4	(17) 4	
(9) 7	(18) 5	

2

(1) 4	(10) 5	(19) 7
(2) 7	(11) 6	(20) 9
(3) 4	(12) 5	(21) 8
(4) 8	(13) 7	(22) 8
(5) 5	(14) 6	(23) 7
(6) 6	(15) 9	(24) 9
(7) 8	(16) 8	(25) 9
(8) 7	(17) 8	
(9) 9	(18) 6	

16 Division
pp 32, 33

1

(1) 7	(10) 4	(19) 7
(2) 4	(11) 6	(20) 8
(3) 6	(12) 5	(21) 4
(4) 5	(13) 4	(22) 5
(5) 7	(14) 9	(23) 7
(6) 8	(15) 8	(24) 9
(7) 6	(16) 6	(25) 8
(8) 4	(17) 5	
(9) 5	(18) 6	

2

(1) 4	(10) 7	(19) 9
(2) 6	(11) 4	(20) 8
(3) 6	(12) 5	(21) 9
(4) 3	(13) 3	(22) 6
(5) 7	(14) 6	(23) 5
(6) 8	(15) 5	(24) 8
(7) 7	(16) 9	(25) 7
(8) 6	(17) 9	
(9) 5	(18) 7	

17 Division

pp 34, 35

1
(1) 7	(10) 8	(19) 9
(2) 9	(11) 4	(20) 7
(3) 5	(12) 6	(21) 9
(4) 4	(13) 5	(22) 6
(5) 8	(14) 4	(23) 8
(6) 7	(15) 6	(24) 8
(7) 5	(16) 5	(25) 9
(8) 9	(17) 7	
(9) 6	(18) 7	

2
(1) 7	(10) 9	(19) 5
(2) 7	(11) 9	(20) 7
(3) 7	(12) 4	(21) 9
(4) 6	(13) 8	(22) 8
(5) 9	(14) 7	(23) 6
(6) 8	(15) 8	(24) 5
(7) 8	(16) 6	(25) 9
(8) 8	(17) 9	
(9) 7	(18) 6	

18 Division with Remainders

pp 36, 37

1
- (1) 4 ÷ 2 = 2 ⟨Ans.⟩ 2 pieces
- (2) 5 ÷ 2 = 2 R 1 ⟨Ans.⟩ 2 pieces with a remainder of 1
- (3) 6 ÷ 3 = 2 ⟨Ans.⟩ 2 pieces
- (4) 7 ÷ 3 = 2 R 1 ⟨Ans.⟩ 2 pieces with a remainder of 1
- (5) 8 ÷ 3 = 2 R 2 ⟨Ans.⟩ 2 pieces with a remainder of 2

2
- (1) 9 ÷ 3 = 3 ⟨Ans.⟩ 3 pieces
- (2) 10 ÷ 3 = 3 R 1 ⟨Ans.⟩ 3 pieces with a remainder of 1
- (3) 11 ÷ 3 = 3 R 2 ⟨Ans.⟩ 3 pieces with a remainder of 2
- (4) 11 ÷ 4 = 2 R 3 ⟨Ans.⟩ 2 pieces with a remainder of 3
- (5) 13 ÷ 4 = 3 R 1 ⟨Ans.⟩ 3 pieces with a remainder of 1
- (6) 14 ÷ 4 = 3 R 2 ⟨Ans.⟩ 3 pieces with a remainder of 2
- (7) 15 ÷ 4 = 3 R 3 ⟨Ans.⟩ 3 pieces with a remainder of 3

19 Division with Remainders

pp 38, 39

1
(1) 2	(10) 6 R 1	(19) 3 R 1
(2) 2 R 1	(11) 7	(20) 5
(3) 3	(12) 7 R 1	(21) 5 R 1
(4) 3 R 1	(13) 8	(22) 6
(5) 4	(14) 8 R 1	(23) 7 R 1
(6) 4 R 1	(15) 9	(24) 8
(7) 5	(16) 9 R 1	(25) 8 R 1
(8) 5 R 1	(17) 2 R 1	
(9) 6	(18) 3	

2
(1) 2	(10) 5	(19) 8
(2) 2 R 1	(11) 5 R 1	(20) 8 R 1
(3) 2 R 2	(12) 5 R 2	(21) 8 R 2
(4) 3	(13) 6	(22) 9
(5) 3 R 1	(14) 6 R 1	(23) 9 R 1
(6) 3 R 2	(15) 6 R 2	(24) 9 R 2
(7) 4	(16) 7	(25) 4 R 1
(8) 4 R 1	(17) 7 R 1	
(9) 4 R 2	(18) 7 R 2	

20 Division with Remainders

pp 40, 41

1
(1) 2	(10) 5	(19) 7 R 1
(2) 2 R 1	(11) 4	(20) 8
(3) 2 R 2	(12) 4 R 1	(21) 6
(4) 3	(13) 4 R 2	(22) 6 R 1
(5) 3 R 1	(14) 5	(23) 6 R 2
(6) 3	(15) 5 R 1	(24) 7
(7) 3 R 1	(16) 6	(25) 7 R 1
(8) 4	(17) 6 R 1	
(9) 4 R 1	(18) 7	

2
(1) 2	(10) 4 R 1	(19) 6 R 3
(2) 2 R 1	(11) 4 R 2	(20) 7
(3) 2 R 2	(12) 4 R 3	(21) 7 R 2
(4) 2 R 3	(13) 5	(22) 8 R 1
(5) 3	(14) 5 R 1	(23) 9
(6) 3 R 1	(15) 5 R 2	(24) 9 R 2
(7) 3 R 2	(16) 5 R 3	(25) 9 R 3
(8) 3 R 3	(17) 6	
(9) 4	(18) 6 R 1	

21 Division with Remainders

pp 42, 43

1
(1) 2	(10) 3 R 4	(19) 6 R 3
(2) 2 R 1	(11) 4	(20) 7 R 1
(3) 2 R 2	(12) 4 R 1	(21) 7 R 4
(4) 2 R 3	(13) 4 R 2	(22) 8 R 2
(5) 2 R 4	(14) 4 R 3	(23) 9
(6) 3	(15) 5	(24) 9 R 2
(7) 3 R 1	(16) 5 R 2	(25) 9 R 4
(8) 3 R 2	(17) 5 R 4	
(9) 3 R 3	(18) 6	

2
(1) 3	(10) 5	(19) 7 R 3
(2) 3 R 1	(11) 4	(20) 8
(3) 3 R 2	(12) 4 R 1	(21) 5
(4) 3 R 3	(13) 4 R 2	(22) 5 R 1
(5) 3 R 4	(14) 4 R 3	(23) 5 R 2
(6) 4	(15) 4 R 4	(24) 5 R 3
(7) 4 R 1	(16) 7	(25) 5 R 4
(8) 4 R 2	(17) 7 R 1	
(9) 4 R 3	(18) 7 R 2	

22 Division with Remainders

pp 44, 45

1
(1) 2	(10) 6	(19) 9 R 2
(2) 3 R 1	(11) 7 R 1	(20) 2
(3) 5	(12) 8 R 2	(21) 3 R 1
(4) 6 R 1	(13) 2	(22) 4 R 2
(5) 8	(14) 3 R 1	(23) 5 R 3
(6) 9 R 1	(15) 4 R 2	(24) 6 R 4
(7) 2	(16) 5 R 3	(25) 8
(8) 3 R 1	(17) 7	
(9) 4 R 2	(18) 8 R 1	

2
(1) 2 R 1	(10) 6 R 2	(19) 2 R 2
(2) 4	(11) 8	(20) 3 R 3
(3) 5 R 1	(12) 9 R 1	(21) 4 R 4
(4) 7	(13) 2 R 1	(22) 6
(5) 8 R 1	(14) 3 R 2	(23) 7 R 1
(6) 9 R 1	(15) 4 R 3	(24) 8 R 2
(7) 2 R 2	(16) 6	(25) 9 R 3
(8) 4	(17) 7 R 1	
(9) 5 R 1	(18) 8 R 2	

23 Division with Remainders
pp 46, 47

1
(1) 3	(10) 2 R 1	(19) 2 R 1
(2) 2	(11) 1 R 4	(20) 6
(3) 3 R 1	(12) 5	(21) 4
(4) 2 R 1	(13) 3 R 1	(22) 3
(5) 4	(14) 2 R 2	(23) 2 R 2
(6) 2 R 2	(15) 2	(24) 6 R 1
(7) 2	(16) 5 R 1	(25) 4 R 1
(8) 4 R 1	(17) 3 R 2	
(9) 3	(18) 2 R 3	

2
(1) 6	(10) 2 R 3	(19) 7 R 1
(2) 4	(11) 2 R 1	(20) 5
(3) 3	(12) 1 R 6	(21) 3 R 3
(4) 2 R 2	(13) 7	(22) 3
(5) 2	(14) 4 R 2	(23) 2 R 3
(6) 1 R 5	(15) 3 R 2	(24) 2 R 1
(7) 6 R 1	(16) 2 R 4	(25) 1 R 7
(8) 4 R 1	(17) 2 R 2	
(9) 3 R 1	(18) 2	

24 Division with Remainders
pp 48, 49

1
(1) 8	(10) 5 R 2	(19) 4 R 2
(2) 5 R 1	(11) 4 R 1	(20) 3 R 3
(3) 4	(12) 3 R 2	(21) 3
(4) 3 R 1	(13) 2 R 5	(22) 2 R 4
(5) 2 R 4	(14) 2 R 3	(23) 2 R 2
(6) 2 R 2	(15) 2 R 1	(24) 2
(7) 2	(16) 1 R 8	(25) 9 R 1
(8) 1 R 7	(17) 9	
(9) 8 R 1	(18) 6	

2
(1) 9 R 1	(10) 6 R 2	(19) 5 R 1
(2) 6 R 1	(11) 5	(20) 4 R 1
(3) 4 R 3	(12) 4	(21) 3 R 3
(4) 3 R 4	(13) 3 R 2	(22) 3
(5) 3 R 1	(14) 2 R 6	(23) 2 R 5
(6) 2 R 5	(15) 2 R 4	(24) 2 R 3
(7) 2 R 3	(16) 2 R 2	(25) 7 R 1
(8) 2 R 1	(17) 10	
(9) 10	(18) 7	

25 Division with Remainders
pp 50, 51

1
(1) 7 R 1	(10) 4 R 3	(19) 3 R 3
(2) 5 R 2	(11) 3 R 5	(20) 3
(3) 4 R 2	(12) 3 R 2	(21) 2 R 6
(4) 3 R 4	(13) 2 R 7	(22) 8 R 1
(5) 3 R 1	(14) 2 R 5	(23) 6 R 1
(6) 2 R 6	(15) 8	(24) 5
(7) 2 R 4	(16) 6	(25) 4 R 1
(8) 7 R 2	(17) 4 R 4	
(9) 5 R 3	(18) 4	

2
(1) 8 R 1	(10) 5 R 1	(19) 3 R 6
(2) 6 R 1	(11) 4 R 2	(20) 3 R 3
(3) 5	(12) 3 R 5	(21) 3
(4) 4 R 1	(13) 3 R 2	(22) 9 R 1
(5) 3 R 4	(14) 2 R 8	(23) 7
(6) 3 R 1	(15) 9	(24) 5 R 3
(7) 2 R 7	(16) 6 R 3	(25) 4 R 4
(8) 8 R 2	(17) 5 R 2	
(9) 6 R 2	(18) 4 R 3	

26 Division with Remainders
pp 52, 53

1
(1) 7	(10) 4 R 5	(19) 3 R 6
(2) 5 R 3	(11) 4 R 1	(20) 7 R 3
(3) 4 R 4	(12) 3 R 5	(21) 6 R 1
(4) 4	(13) 3 R 2	(22) 5 R 1
(5) 3 R 4	(14) 10	(23) 4 R 3
(6) 3 R 1	(15) 7 R 2	(24) 3 R 7
(7) 9 R 2	(16) 6	(25) 3 R 4
(8) 7 R 1	(17) 5	
(9) 5 R 4	(18) 4 R 2	

2
(1) 8	(10) 4 R 5	(19) 8 R 3
(2) 6 R 2	(11) 4 R 1	(20) 7
(3) 5 R 2	(12) 3 R 6	(21) 5 R 5
(4) 4 R 4	(13) 8 R 2	(22) 5
(5) 4	(14) 6 R 4	(23) 4 R 3
(6) 3 R 5	(15) 5 R 4	(24) 3 R 8
(7) 8 R 1	(16) 4 R 6	(25) 9
(8) 6 R 3	(17) 4 R 2	
(9) 5 R 3	(18) 3 R 7	

27 Division with Remainders
pp 54, 55

1
(1) 9	(10) 4 R 5	(19) 5 R 4
(2) 7 R 1	(11) 4 R 1	(20) 4 R 7
(3) 6	(12) 7 R 3	(21) 4 R 3
(4) 5 R 1	(13) 6 R 2	(22) 10
(5) 4 R 4	(14) 5 R 3	(23) 8
(6) 4	(15) 4 R 6	(24) 6 R 4
(7) 7 R 2	(16) 4 R 2	(25) 5 R 5
(8) 6 R 1	(17) 7 R 4	
(9) 5 R 2	(18) 6 R 3	

2
(1) 10	(10) 8 R 1	(19) 4 R 6
(2) 8	(11) 6 R 5	(20) 8 R 3
(3) 6 R 4	(12) 5 R 6	(21) 7 R 1
(4) 5 R 5	(13) 5 R 1	(22) 6 R 1
(5) 5	(14) 4 R 5	(23) 5 R 3
(6) 4 R 4	(15) 8 R 2	(24) 4 R 7
(7) 2	(16) 7	(25) 8 R 4
(8) 3	(17) 6	
(9) 4	(18) 5 R 2	

28 Division with Remainders pp 56, 57

1
(1) 8 R 4	(10) 5	(19) 5 R 7
(2) 7 R 2	(11) 9 R 1	(20) 5 R 2
(3) 6 R 2	(12) 7 R 4	(21) 9 R 3
(4) 5 R 4	(13) 6 R 4	(22) 8
(5) 4 R 8	(14) 5 R 6	(23) 6 R 6
(6) 9	(15) 5 R 1	(24) 6
(7) 7 R 3	(16) 9 R 2	(25) 5 R 3
(8) 6 R 3	(17) 7 R 5	
(9) 5 R 5	(18) 6 R 5	

2
(1) 9 R 4	(10) 5 R 5	(19) 7 R 3
(2) 8 R 1	(11) 3	(20) 6 R 4
(3) 7	(12) 4	(21) 5 R 7
(4) 6 R 1	(13) 5	(22) 8 R 5
(5) 5 R 4	(14) 8 R 3	(23) 7 R 4
(6) 10	(15) 7 R 2	(24) 6 R 5
(7) 8 R 2	(16) 6 R 3	(25) 5 R 8
(8) 7 R 1	(17) 5 R 6	
(9) 6 R 2	(18) 8 R 4	

29 Division with Remainders pp 58, 59

1
(1) 9	(10) 8	(19) 7 R 2
(2) 7 R 5	(11) 7	(20) 6 R 4
(3) 6 R 6	(12) 6 R 2	(21) 9 R 5
(4) 6	(13) 9 R 3	(22) 8 R 3
(5) 9 R 1	(14) 8 R 1	(23) 7 R 3
(6) 7 R 6	(15) 7 R 1	(24) 6 R 5
(7) 6 R 7	(16) 6 R 3	(25) 10
(8) 6 R 1	(17) 9 R 4	
(9) 9 R 2	(18) 8 R 2	

2
(1) 10	(10) 6 R 7	(19) 7 R 1
(2) 8 R 4	(11) 8 R 6	(20) 9 R 2
(3) 7 R 4	(12) 7 R 6	(21) 8 R 1
(4) 6 R 6	(13) 6 R 8	(22) 7 R 2
(5) 4	(14) 9	(23) 9 R 3
(6) 5	(15) 7 R 7	(24) 8 R 2
(7) 6	(16) 7	(25) 7 R 3
(8) 8 R 5	(17) 9 R 1	
(9) 7 R 5	(18) 8	

30 Division with Remainders pp 60, 61

1
(1) 9 R 4	(10) 5	(19) 9 R 2
(2) 8 R 3	(11) 6	(20) 8 R 2
(3) 7 R 4	(12) 7	(21) 9 R 3
(4) 9 R 5	(13) 8 R 7	(22) 8 R 3
(5) 8 R 4	(14) 7 R 8	(23) 9 R 4
(6) 7 R 5	(15) 9	(24) 8 R 4
(7) 10	(16) 8	(25) 9 R 5
(8) 8 R 6	(17) 9 R 1	
(9) 7 R 7	(18) 8 R 1	

2
(1) 8 R 3	(10) 10	(19) 9 R 5
(2) 9 R 4	(11) 8 R 8	(20) 9 R 6
(3) 8 R 4	(12) 6	(21) 9 R 7
(4) 9 R 5	(13) 7	(22) 9 R 8
(5) 8 R 5	(14) 8	(23) 10
(6) 9 R 6	(15) 9	(24) 8
(7) 8 R 6	(16) 9 R 1	(25) 9
(8) 9 R 7	(17) 9 R 3	
(9) 8 R 7	(18) 9 R 4	

31 Division with Remainders pp 62, 63

1
(1) 5 R 1	(10) 10	(19) 4 R 3
(2) 4 R 2	(11) 4 R 3	(20) 4
(3) 3 R 5	(12) 4	(21) 8 R 1
(4) 3 R 3	(13) 3 R 6	(22) 7
(5) 3 R 1	(14) 8 R 2	(23) 6 R 1
(6) 2 R 8	(15) 7	(24) 5 R 4
(7) 9	(16) 6	(25) 5
(8) 7	(17) 5 R 2	
(9) 5 R 4	(18) 4 R 6	

2
(1) 7 R 1	(10) 7 R 2	(19) 6 R 6
(2) 8 R 1	(11) 6 R 3	(20) 9 R 2
(3) 6 R 4	(12) 5 R 6	(21) 7 R 2
(4) 8 R 3	(13) 5 R 2	(22) 6 R 4
(5) 4 R 5	(14) 7	(23) 7 R 3
(6) 4 R 2	(15) 5	(24) 6 R 5
(7) 5 R 6	(16) 6 R 3	(25) 10
(8) 5 R 2	(17) 5 R 7	
(9) 4 R 7	(18) 7 R 4	

32 Division with Remainders pp 64, 65

1
(1) 10	(10) 8	(19) 7 R 7
(2) 8	(11) 7	(20) 8 R 7
(3) 6 R 5	(12) 10	(21) 9
(4) 6	(13) 6	(22) 8 R 1
(5) 5 R 3	(14) 9 R 4	(23) 9 R 2
(6) 4 R 8	(15) 8 R 4	(24) 8 R 3
(7) 9	(16) 9 R 6	(25) 9 R 2
(8) 7 R 3	(17) 7 R 6	
(9) 9 R 2	(18) 10	

②
(1) 7 R 2   (10) 9 R 2   (19) 8 R 1
(2) 8 R 4   (11) 7 R 4   (20) 9 R 2
(3) 5 R 8   (12) 8 R 4   (21) 8 R 3
(4) 6 R 6   (13) 7 R 6   (22) 9 R 6
(5) 8   (14) 8 R 6   (23) 9
(6) 7 R 1   (15) 7 R 7   (24) 9 R 2
(7) 6 R 4   (16) 7   (25) 9 R 5
(8) 6 R 7   (17) 7 R 8
(9) 7 R 6   (18) 9

㉝ Division with Remainders   pp 66,67

①
(1) 7 R 1   (10) 10   (19) 2 R 2
(2) 3 R 3   (11) 4 R 4   (20) 2 R 2
(3) 6 R 3   (12) 4 R 2   (21) 6 R 1
(4) 5 R 1   (13) 3 R 8   (22) 7 R 3
(5) 4 R 4   (14) 10   (23) 3 R 6
(6) 2 R 6   (15) 4 R 8   (24) 3
(7) 5 R 2   (16) 8   (25) 5 R 2
(8) 5 R 1   (17) 4 R 2
(9) 7 R 1   (18) 5 R 4

②
(1) 5 R 5   (10) 7 R 2   (19) 7
(2) 8 R 4   (11) 10   (20) 6 R 4
(3) 7 R 8   (12) 9 R 1   (21) 7
(4) 9 R 3   (13) 7 R 1   (22) 9 R 4
(5) 9   (14) 6 R 6   (23) 8 R 6
(6) 6 R 7   (15) 8 R 4   (24) 7 R 4
(7) 5 R 2   (16) 7 R 5   (25) 7 R 2
(8) 9 R 4   (17) 8 R 1
(9) 9 R 3   (18) 9 R 5

㉞ Vertical Form Division   pp 68,69

① $10 \div 2 = 5$ $2\overline{)10}$ → 5

②
(1) $2\overline{)12}$ → 6   (7) $3\overline{)27}$ → 9   (13) 4
(2) $2\overline{)16}$ → 8   (8) $4\overline{)12}$ → 3   (14) 7
(3) $2\overline{)18}$ → 9   (9) $4\overline{)20}$ → 5   (15) 8
(4) $3\overline{)12}$ → 4   (10) $4\overline{)28}$ → 7   (16) 2
(5) $3\overline{)15}$ → 5   (11) $4\overline{)36}$ → 9   (17) 3
(6) $3\overline{)18}$ → 6   (12) $5\overline{)15}$ → 3   (18) 5

③
(1) 2   (8) 6   (15) 9
(2) 4   (9) 4   (16) 6
(3) 5   (10) 2   (17) 4
(4) 3   (11) 8   (18) 8
(5) 5   (12) 6   (19) 6
(6) 2   (13) 4   (20) 5
(7) 4   (14) 3

㉟ Vertical Form Division   pp 70,71

① $14 \div 3 = 4$ R 2 $3\overline{)14}$ → 4 R 2

②
(1) $2\overline{)14}$ → 7   (7) $4\overline{)26}$ → 6 R 2   (13) 4
(2) $2\overline{)15}$ → 7 R 1   (8) $4\overline{)27}$ → 6 R 3   (14) 4 R 2
(3) $3\overline{)15}$ → 5   (9) $5\overline{)25}$ → 5   (15) 4
(4) $3\overline{)16}$ → 5 R 1   (10) $5\overline{)28}$ → 5 R 3   (16) 4 R 4
(5) $3\overline{)17}$ → 5 R 2   (11) $6\overline{)24}$ → 4   (17) 4
(6) $4\overline{)24}$ → 6   (12) $6\overline{)27}$ → 4 R 3   (18) 4 R 2

③
(1) 8   (8) 5 R 3   (15) 6
(2) 8 R 1   (9) 6   (16) 6 R 3
(3) 6   (10) 6 R 1   (17) 6
(4) 6 R 1   (11) 6 R 4   (18) 6 R 2
(5) 6 R 2   (12) 6   (19) 6
(6) 5   (13) 6 R 1   (20) 6 R 3
(7) 5 R 2   (14) 6 R 4

㊱ Vertical Form Division   pp 72,73

①
(1) 8   (8) 8 R 1   (15) 4 R 4
(2) 5 R 1   (9) 6 R 1   (16) 8
(3) 4   (10) 5   (17) 6 R 2
(4) 3 R 1   (11) 9   (18) 5 R 2
(5) 6 R 2   (12) 6 R 3   (19) 4 R 4
(6) 5   (13) 7   (20) 4
(7) 3 R 2   (14) 5 R 3

②
(1) 9   (8) 5 R 5   (15) 9 R 2
(2) 7 R 1   (9) 5   (16) 8
(3) 6   (10) 4 R 4   (17) 7
(4) 5 R 1   (11) 8   (18) 6 R 2
(5) 4 R 4   (12) 6 R 6   (19) 9
(6) 8   (13) 6   (20) 7 R 7
(7) 6 R 4   (14) 5 R 3

37 Vertical Form Division pp 74,75

1
(1) $\dfrac{12}{2\overline{)24}}$ (8) $\dfrac{15}{2\overline{)30}}$ (15) $\dfrac{14}{3\overline{)42}}$

(2) $\dfrac{14}{2\overline{)28}}$ (9) $\dfrac{16}{2\overline{)32}}$ (16) $\dfrac{16}{3\overline{)48}}$

(3) $\dfrac{21}{2\overline{)42}}$ (10) $\dfrac{17}{2\overline{)34}}$ (17) $\dfrac{18}{3\overline{)54}}$

(4) $\dfrac{12}{3\overline{)36}}$ (11) $\dfrac{18}{2\overline{)36}}$ (18) $\dfrac{24}{3\overline{)72}}$

(5) $\dfrac{11}{3\overline{)33}}$ (12) $\dfrac{25}{2\overline{)50}}$ (19) $\dfrac{27}{3\overline{)81}}$

(6) $\dfrac{20}{3\overline{)60}}$ (13) $\dfrac{26}{2\overline{)52}}$ (20) $\dfrac{33}{3\overline{)99}}$

(7) $\dfrac{31}{3\overline{)93}}$ (14) $\dfrac{28}{2\overline{)56}}$

2
(1) 8   (8) 3   (15) 14
(2) 12   (9) 15   (16) 15
(3) 17   (10) 12 (17) 26
(4) 11   (11) 16 (18) 17
(5) 12   (12) 5   (19) 13
(6) 13   (13) 11 (20) 27
(7) 18   (14) 12

38 Vertical Form Division pp 76,77

1
(1) 28   (8) 20   (15) 33
(2) 14   (9) 15   (16) 11
(3) 8   (10) 12 (17) 34
(4) 7   (11) 32 (18) 17
(5) 19   (12) 16 (19) 35
(6) 29   (13) 8   (20) 14
(7) 30   (14) 13

2
(1) 39   (8) 12   (15) 23
(2) 26   (9) 45   (16) 32
(3) 13   (10) 30 (17) 24
(4) 27   (11) 18 (18) 12
(5) 9   (12) 15 (19) 33
(6) 28   (13) 10 (20) 11
(7) 14   (14) 46

39 Division of Large Numbers pp 78,79

1
(1) 30   (8) 20   (15) 20
(2) 20   (9) 70   (16) 90
(3) 40   (10) 20 (17) 60
(4) 20   (11) 50 (18) 20
(5) 30   (12) 30 (19) 50
(6) 20   (13) 80 (20) 40
(7) 40   (14) 40

2
(1) 70   (8) 80   (15) 80
(2) 30   (9) 40   (16) 70
(3) 80   (10) 70 (17) 60
(4) 30   (11) 90 (18) 80
(5) 90   (12) 60 (19) 70
(6) 40   (13) 50 (20) 90
(7) 50   (14) 70

40 Division of Large Numbers pp 80,81

1
(1) 300   (11) 200
(2) 200   (12) 500
(3) 400   (13) 300
(4) 200   (14) 800
(5) 300   (15) 400
(6) 500   (16) 200
(7) 200   (17) 900
(8) 400   (18) 600
(9) 300   (19) 300
(10) 700 (20) 200

2
(1) 500   (11) 500
(2) 400   (12) 900
(3) 700   (13) 600
(4) 600   (14) 500
(5) 400   (15) 700
(6) 900   (16) 900
(7) 300   (17) 600
(8) 400   (18) 600
(9) 600   (19) 900
(10) 800 (20) 900

41 Division of Large Numbers pp 82,83

1
(1) 3   (8) 3 R 10   (15) 2 R 50
(2) 2   (9) 2 R 20   (16) 6
(3) 4   (10) 3   (17) 4 R 20
(4) 2 R 20   (11) 2 R 20   (18) 4
(5) 4 R 10   (12) 5   (19) 3 R 20
(6) 3   (13) 3 R 30   (20) 2 R 60
(7) 5   (14) 3 R 10

2
(1) 6   (8) 6   (15) 8 R 20
(2) 4 R 40   (9) 5 R 50   (16) 9
(3) 4   (10) 7   (17) 7 R 50
(4) 3 R 40   (11) 7 R 30   (18) 8 R 40
(5) 4   (12) 5 R 50   (19) 7 R 40
(6) 3 R 50   (13) 5   (20) 7 R 70
(7) 7 R 10   (14) 5 R 30

42 Division of Large Numbers pp 84,85

1
(1) 3   (11) 2
(2) 2   (12) 5
(3) 6   (13) 3
(4) 4   (14) 8
(5) 2   (15) 4
(6) 5   (16) 9
(7) 2   (17) 3
(8) 4   (18) 2
(9) 3   (19) 5
(10) 2   (20) 4

2
(1) 7   (11) 4
(2) 8   (12) 5
(3) 6   (13) 6
(4) 9   (14) 5
(5) 4   (15) 6
(6) 6   (16) 9
(7) 8   (17) 8
(8) 4   (18) 9
(9) 5   (19) 8
(10) 9   (20) 8

(43) Review

1
(1) 9	(7) 6	(13) 7
(2) 2	(8) 8	(14) 8
(3) 5	(9) 4	(15) 7
(4) 3	(10) 7	(16) 9
(5) 7	(11) 6	
(6) 5	(12) 6	

2
(1) 3	(5) 4	(9) 6
(2) 2 R 2	(6) 3 R 3	(10) 5 R 2
(3) 6	(7) 5 R 5	(11) 6 R 6
(4) 4 R 2	(8) 5	(12) 6

3
(1) 6 R 2	(11) 9	(21) 5 R 4
(2) 7 R 2	(12) 8 R 3	(22) 7 R 6
(3) 2 R 1	(13) 8 R 8	(23) 7
(4) 7 R 5	(14) 9 R 2	(24) 9 R 3
(5) 8	(15) 10	(25) 8
(6) 7 R 1	(16) 2 R 2	(26) 8 R 6
(7) 7	(17) 7 R 2	(27) 8 R 2
(8) 6 R 1	(18) 7	(28) 8 R 6
(9) 8 R 4	(19) 9 R 1	(29) 9 R 5
(10) 5 R 3	(20) 10	(30) 6 R 6

4
(1) 70	(4) 8 R 60
(2) 80	(5) 3 R 10
(3) 8	(6) 2 R 50

Advice

If you made many mistakes in **1**, start reviewing on page 16.

If you made many mistakes in **2** or **3**, start reviewing on page 36.

If you made many mistakes in **4**, start reviewing on page 78.